Triumphant Transitions

**CHRISTOPHER H. MCKINNEY, SR.
& HENRY L. HAYES, JR.**

Triumphant Transitions
Trilogy Christian Publishers A Wholly Owned Subsidiary of Trinity
Broadcasting Network
2442 Michelle Drive Tustin, CA 92780
Trilogy Christian Publishing/TBN and colophon are trademarks of Trinity
Broadcasting Network. For information about special discounts for bulk
purchases, please contact Trilogy Christian Publishing.
Trilogy Disclaimer: The views and content expressed in this book are those
of the author and may not necessarily reflect the views and doctrine of
Trilogy Christian Publishing or the Trinity Broadcasting Network.
Cover design by: Kelly Stewart
Manufactured in the United States of America
10 9 8 7 6 5 4 3 2 1
Library of Congress Cataloging-in-Publication Data is available.
ISBN: 978-1-68556-298-4
E-ISBN: 978-1-68556-299-1

DO EXCEPTIONALLY WELL IN THE JOB THAT
YOU ARE DOING, WHILE TAKING BABY STEPS
TOWARDS YOUR FUTURE. THAT PREVENTS YOU
FROM HAVING TO SPRINT TOWARDS THE END!

FOREWARD

This is one of those books I wished would have been written a decade ago when I was making my transition from military to civilian life. It is quite frankly a treasure map that will take anyone to their life's treasure. I can't help thinking what my life would have been like if I had this resource.

Professionally I have led, mentored, and served thousands of military members and their families for over 30 years in the United States Air Force. Since retiring from the military, I was the program director for a mental health program, deputy director for health services for the South Carolina Department of Corrections and now I am the director of support services for the City of Sumter. I have become an international bestselling author four times and have given a TEDx Talk that has garnered over 550,000 views. I have gained a great experience and have had great success.

But this isn't the full tale. If we go back to January 2012, it was a totally different story. I remember when I was notified by the Air Force Personnel Center that I was eligible for retirement. I was blown away. I never really seriously thought about it, never took my transition seriously. Up to the age of 17 the only house I knew was my parents' house. At

17 I left my parents' house and went into Uncle Sam's house. All I knew in my adult life was the military. I did not know how to be a civilian. I didn't even speak like a civilian. Like many, I had the opportunity to go through the Transition Assistance Program (TAP), and I was also blessed to go to Chief's TAP, but I had waited until I had less than a year left in the service. I wish I would have had this book, *Triumphant Transitions*, in my hands when it was my turn to move. Chris and Henry, two great men, great friends, and great leaders, have put together a roadmap for your success. To paraphrase a passage from my favorite book, "A lamp to your feet and a light to your path" (Psalm 119:105). These leaders have made successful transitions and have had the integrity to write a book for those who come behind them.

Not only have Chris and Henry reached the highest levels of the Air Force Enlisted Corps, but they also have both achieved high positions in the civilian sector. Speaking from experience, the positions they have achieved were not easy to come by. They are responsible for large and diverse organizations and millions of dollars. The decisions they make are of enormous impact. In this powerful work they have given tools and principles that will prepare you to take the next steps towards your dreams and careers. They lay out a framework and mindset that, if followed, will lead you towards wherever you are willing to go.

In my career, and in many training situations, I have learned a great deal; but to be honest, much of my learning came during "sidebar" conversations. These are the conversations where we took the time to fuss, cuss, and discuss to the point of understanding. What makes this book so powerful is that you will get a great mental model for success, examples of how it was done right and sometimes wrong, and finally, as the great Paul Harvey use to say, "the rest of the story."

I am honored to write this forward, and I know that this book will change your life for the better. In the following pages you will be led through valuable lessons that will help you to move confidently from where you are to where you desire to be.

Chris and Henry are wonderful authors and dear friends that will help you triumphantly transition. I pray that you take their words to heart and that you will be blessed by the experience.

Here is to your successful transition, may the rest of your days be the best of your days!

Lefford L. Fate
Support Services Director, City of Sumter
Command Chief Master Sergeant (Ret.)
TEDx Speaker (550K views)
Author of Correcting Corrections
Co-Author of Pathway to a Positive Mental Attitude and P.E.R.S.I.S.T.E.N.C.E.

PREFACE

So why should you read this book? Why should you spend your hard-earned money on this particular product? Fair questions. The bottom line is we have something of value to offer you. This book is a collaboration between two individuals who both entered the military at an entry level position. By GOD's grace and favor and a lot of blood, sweat, tears, and intentional personal growth both ascended to the rank of Chief Master Sergeant. This is the top 1% of our branch of military service.

In recent history, only approximately .5% of the U.S. population serves in the defense of our country (years ago it used to be 1%). Of that .5%, approximately 24% of them are in the Air Force, meaning 0.12% of the country serve as Airmen. Then of that 0.12%, 80% are enlisted showing that 0.096% of our nation are enlisted Airmen. And of that 0.096%, we had the privilege to be a part of the top 1%, revealing that Chiefs are 0.00097% or one one-thousandth of a percent of our great nation. This is not meant to be braggadocious, but merely to give context.

Both of us also had the privilege to steward the office of the Command Chief (top 1% of the top 1%) at different installations, meaning we were a part of the base executive branch. One transitioned to be the Chief Administrative Officer (Town Manager) of a very prosperous town in Massachusetts and the other to be the Chief Executive Officer (Executive Director) for a regional planning and development agency for four-counties in South Carolina. Both transitions are *not* the typical transitions for an enlisted person. One of us is 1 ½ years into the transition and the other 4 years. By the grace and favor of GOD and a lot more blood, sweat, tears, and intentional personal growth, we each are not just surviving in our new career paths, but thriving. We each have achieved some significant accomplishments by translating our experiences from our former careers to our new teams in the local government sector.

If you personally knew someone that has ascended to the top 1% of any field, I would hope you would have coffee or tea with them on a regular basis to glean insight. Then if you knew someone who ascended to the top 1% of the top 1%, I would guess it would also be worth your while to buy them a cup of coffee and chat. Our intent with this book is to sit down with you and have coffee or tea and share insights that we are confident will help you to make a successful transition, be it from being a senior in college to the workforce, the military to civilian life, an educator to corporate America, frontline worker to manager, a senior in high school to college or from being a stay at home mom or dad to being an entrepreneur. It doesn't matter what your transition may be, we are confident this book will help! In transition, there are some basic things that remain constant. It is our intent to provide you with a nugget or two that will help you transition and see the same or greater success as in your previous endeavors.

Blessings,

Mac & HH

ACKNOWLEDGMENTS

We want to thank our families for being so supportive and patient with us throughout this process. We both got caught working on this book during vacation and other sensitive times, however, the encouragement we received along the way really empowered and motivated us to keep going. May this work be a blessing to our own children and their friends, you have heard some of our discussions about the subject of triumphant transitions on many occasions. Hopefully you will get the principles embedded within you and accelerate the preparation for future opportunities!

To Danya and Stephanie, your loving feedback, as well as your cues and signals on when it is time to shut it down, helped to maintain a measure of balance along the way. You are the very reason for our constant efforts to be better, do better and help others get better. You have our unyielding, insatiable love!

— Chris and Henry

INTRODUCTION

WE CANNOT CHANGE ANYTHING UNTIL WE ACCEPT IT. CONDEMNATION DOES NOT LIBERATE, IT OPPRESSES.

- Carl Jung

Transition (change) is inevitable, so why do we fight it and try to avoid it? Transition (change) "happens" to and with us all, so why not acknowledge, accept, and anticipate it? If we want to have any measure of success, we are going to face the truth in transition (change): transition (change) is going to happen anyway, so relax. Why try to avoid it or fight it? If we embrace the inevitable transition (change), prepare for the transition (change) and make the necessary personal adjustments, transition (change) can end well.

If you are in line with your purpose or passion, it is possible to launch into something much more fulfilling by seeking spiritual solutions; building on past successes; watching, working and praying; defeating double-mindedness (let your eye be single); press past the past (it should bless, not stress you); get after the gap; naysayers say so; identify your entities (fire-lighters, fire fighters, and fire pits); expect the exceptional (grace, mercy, and favor of GOD and man); your steps are ordered – do your part (must be faith filled movement, stretch forth your hand); how bad do you want it; run through the end; victory laps and trophies (gratefulness to GOD); build the next team of champions.

There is a statement by Marshall Goldsmith that deeply resonates within me, "What got you here won't get you there." It is a powerful and encouraging, yet intimidating thought. The previous successes are not enough to propel you into the next phase or era. Some of the skills are not transferable in their original form. What adjustments are necessary?

Preparation is a process. Discipline and determination are drivers.

CONTENTS

Develop a Deliberate Plan

Get After It Consistently

Reevaluate and Reassess

Mind the Gaps & Mine the Gaps

Know Up Front Some Won't Be Supportive

Guard Your Heart

Don't Take It Personally

Shopping Cart Method

Fire Fighters

Fire Lighters

Fire Pits

What is Networking

Get Past Your Feelings

Take People at Their Word

Networking Tools

Quick Tips On Connecting With People You Do Not Know

Connections, Mentors/Coaches, Sponsor, Friends

Clean Up Your Online Presence

1.

CHANGE
IS
GOING
TO
HAPPEN
ANYWAY...

GET
GOOD
AT
IT!

Psst...can we talk? For real, can we talk about change? How about change related to you? Change is another way to label something as being different or a shift occurring. Throughout your entire life, shift happens!

As a matter of fact, you can champion change in many prominent ways. Who really wants their child to stay in diapers for 20 years? What about remaining in high school forever? Or, for a person to maintain a static intellectual level? How about staying in the same job and pay grade for 32 years? Although these things are not desirable in general, they prove that we need change in our lives.

If you are a person gaining education and stacking understanding and wisdom, you are seeking change. But for what purpose? Your desire to get a promotion or new position is the quest for change. Every time that I heard someone say that they just want to make it so far in a job or life, I wondered if they really meant it and why.

So, if change is going to happen, why not prepare for it, like you do in other areas of life? In order to have a triumphant transition, it is best to approach it with a solid plan and intention. And then work the plan! Hope is not a plan; a plan is not action. Said differently, faith without work is dead. There are no rewards for immobility.

I bet you've heard it said that you can be anything you want to be in life. It was probably said by a loved one. I do not subscribe to that logic. I say that you can become what you prepare for and have a valid opportunity. Preparation leads to readiness for change. Sitting still won't project you into a posture of progress!

That reminds me, I've been known to say that "stagnation is death." To be clear, an adverse impact may not occur for everyone in the same way or at the same time, but it does occur. Imagine this: a planter is sitting in the grass. Everything is fresh, vibrant, and smells great. The lawn is well manicured. Much attention is given to grow and fertilize the flowers contained therein. Spring and summer produce considerable beauty.

One day, the maintenance crew moves the planter. What is discovered? In all of the splendor, underneath the planter was a dead spot. Because there was no movement through the seasons, the connection point became evidence of stagnation. This created an undeniable difference in what was and what could be. If only the planter's location had changed at the right time, at the right interval or to the right place, death may have been avoidable. A key point in this is the death did not occur immediately. It was a slow process of perishing.

Despite the glory of the top and inside of the pot, what it was directly connected to, in an obscure way, died. Did you catch that? It looks good, smells good, and is good. And still stagnation produced death.

What is connected to you that is on the path of destruction because you are not changing? Could you be stunting the growth of those in your house? What pattern are you projecting for those following you? How are you impacting your siblings who look up to you?

Change is going to happen, so get good at it! I didn't say you had to like or love it. Just get good at it. When you were a child, you thought as a child. And when you got older, you put away childish things. Expecting life to hand you ease and comfort in every area is unrealistic. Being diligent in your preparation will help out when challenges arise.

"EVERYBODY HAS A PLAN UNTIL THEY GET PUNCHED IN THE MOUTH."

-Iron Mike Tyson [1]

Let's listen to what the Champ, Mike Tyson, is and isn't saying…

• **Everyone has a plan:** Failure to plan is ludicrous! We have to make plans. It establishes pathways that may lead to successes. I did not guarantee success. You have heard it said that failure to plan is planning to fail. I agree to an extent. Success can still occur, you just may not have realized the path you were on. And unfortunately, you may not be able to articulate it to those that want to follow your footsteps. Intent of outcome is one thing, plans are another.

• **… until they get punched in the mouth:** Something will attempt to knock you off of your game plan. Do you have what it takes to stay in the fight? Did you come to the ring with only one thought? Are you under-prepared for the encounters you face? Transition is a contact sport, and sometimes people get hurt. Are you prepared for the first hit you may take?

Don't fold under the pressure, you can take it! In your prep time, include dealing with rejection, disappointment, and betrayal. If you rehearse the situation before you encounter it, the impact and reactions should not be as damaging. Like the reason boxers spar with types and styles similar to their next opponent. The goal is to reduce the potential elements of surprise and temper the competitor to the pain management or tolerance needed to keep pressing forward.

Does the potential for pain management (or tolerance) occur in job seeking? Absolutely! It will help with your emotional health and well-being. If you allow yourself to get unnecessarily disturbed, it could allow discontentment and despair to creep in. You must guard against this. One way to reinforce proper thinking is to listen to the wisdom of my grandmother, she would say, "Give time time, baby. It'll change."

2.

PURPOSE AND PASSION ARE PROJECTING AND PROTECTING

In 2006-2007 I had a conversation with two senior leaders. One encounter I think of as a drive-by mentorship. I was asked a question and before I could provide an answer, I was told what I should do in order to accelerate my promotion likelihood. The thing is his advice was structurally sound and would produce the results desired in most cases. But I didn't feel that I wanted to follow through with those actions. You see, I didn't feel as if it was time to go back to my previous area of expertise. I thought I was supposed to move from repairing airplanes to empowering people. The thought of going back to aircraft maintenance was fine, the appeal of advancement was exhilarating. The only problem was, I thought I found part of why I was there was for human capital development.

What surprised me was when I spoke with another leader that asked me a question and he waited for the response, evaluated my pattern of actions that he observed and noted the guidance from the other leader. He essentially told me to never chase a penny or position, rather, chase purpose and passion. This lit my fire!

Over the years, my assessment of the word passion has shifted. Many people associate passion with intense desire, to which I don't disagree. Yet, the other side of passion includes an unyielding emotion. Either way, the employment of passion will not produce one getting weary in the pursuit of the goal. It is easy to imagine chasing something you love, but aiming your energy to rectify something you loathe is also noteworthy. You won't tire of either.

An example is a person that has a family ravaged by a certain disease. As a child, they see the damage it causes and internally they make a vow to try to eradicate that destructive force from hurting other families. The fuel towards the quest is more powerful than the work ahead. This is passion.

Purpose comes into the picture when someone is "built for" a certain thing, or "called to" a certain mission, and they know it. When you recognize what you are placed on earth to accomplish, you should strive to grow in and go in that direction. The inner fulfillment will be without comparison! If you cannot stop thinking about a certain functionality in life, explore it. If the momentum draws you deeper, why would you fight it? You may discover an entirely different direction to go in after you have spent 23 years doing something seemingly unrelated. Your age and stage in life is not the biggest question. The biggest question is will you do or become 'that'? What would your life be like if you did it? Better yet, what will be the impact on the lives of others? Or, who will be held back or continue to suffer if you don't step up? Discovering purpose is not something for older people as they near retirement age. If this revelation occurs earlier in life, just imagine how much more could be accomplished.

Understanding your purpose and/or passion is critical to having triumphant transitions. Think about it. What is going to hold you when you are nervous, disappointed, confused, anxious, upset or just ready to give up? Purpose and passion will prevent you from jumping into something that you may despise or that in which your endurance may wane. The absence of understanding your purpose in that area may allow you to resign from a job and subsequently, you take another position because it pays well enough, but you discover you don't feel fulfilled. Then the pressure kicks in again and maybe this is the beginning of a cycle of starting and stopping jobs within a rather short period of time. If you do this too often, your next interviewer may not see you as a stable candidate.

Being centered can help to project you as well as protect you along the way. Projection occurs because the focus can serve as an accelerant, meant to boost you in a given direction. Protection is available, as it can prevent errant exploration. If you can avoid going down a fruitless path, why not save the time, effort, and unproductive energy. This is critically important for everyone. For those transitioning from high school to college, or from college to the workplace, how much time, effort, and money could be saved? How many college students have wasted countless dollars on a degree they do not desire or will not use? Time is a precious commodity that is unable to be reclaimed once it is lost. Preserving and having beneficial uses of your time will turn out to protect you from certain pains and pressure points.

It is our sincere prayer that you and every other reader of this book come into the knowledge of your purpose and passion, at an early stage of your life and/or transition phases. May your heart be enlightened, your mind be engaged, and your soul be refreshed and resilient through your transitions within your lives. This is a focus on employment, yet the principles are applicable to all of life's changes.

3.

DEFEAT DOUBLE-MINDEDNESS

Have you heard that "a double-minded man is unstable in all his ways" (James 1:8)? What is a double-minded man? For the purposes of this book when the term is used, it means vacillating between two thoughts. Science has proven that it is impossible to have two separate thoughts at the same time. If you don't believe me, then try it. Try to have the thought that I am happy, and I am sad at the same time. Okay, so what is the point? That is the point. You can't have two thoughts at the same time, so leverage all of your mental faculties, both conscious and subconscious, on the windshield. The windshield refers to what is in front of you, where you are going. When we look in the rearview mirror, we focus on the past (our current or previous career). What is it that you desire to do? Where do you desire to go? Intentionally focus your thoughts in this direction on this one thing and allow your mind to go to work on your behalf.

The first time you attempt to focus your mind on the transition, it may seem like a very daunting task because the neuro pathways do not have an established path to lead you to success in your new endeavor. The roads have yet to be forged and forging roads is not for the faint of heart. It is hard, painstaking, and exhausting work. The pathway from where you are now to where you desire to go seems like an impossible and implausible task. I get it. I've been there. But the truth is, if you look back to the very beginning of your current career, be that when your first child was born or when you entered college as a freshman, you did not have the neuropathways you presently possess that have helped to make you very successful at what you do. You built each neuropathway one at a time and with the use of each pathway on a regular basis, you went from having a foot trail to creating an interstate system.

It is easy now because of all of the intentional focus and effort you applied to get good at what you are doing. As you look at where you want to be it is just a matter of creating the pathways. This requires intentional, deliberate focus, learning and practice on your part. For me, as someone who had no military background, when I entered the military, I was a student of process at every single step. I did the hard work of learning "new." You did as well, so let's pull the belt tight and get started.

Now I want to share a story that really challenged my single-minded focus. At the time of my transition, my wife and I had an 18, 5 and 3 year old in the house. As we inched closer to September 1, 2017, I felt like my wife had some anxiousness creeping in. From my perspective, it was due in large part to I had not acquired a job. She was very supportive of my pursuit of the one job I felt was where I was supposed to be, but from our conversations I interpreted she was concerned about being able to take care of her babies.

Now she knew that if I had to get three pieces of a job to take care of my family I would, but my short runway had now created a distraction for me. Our intentional arrangement was I was the primary breadwinner, which gave her flexibility. I needed to be able to take care of our needs and being employed was a key component. August rolled around and she would make casual innuendo about if I was seeking employment with any other companies. The middle of August rolled around just as we were preparing to move off base and the casual innuendo became more direct questions and rightfully so, as she wanted some security that the lifestyle she knew was not in jeopardy. I had a responsibility I needed to fulfill.

Truth in lending, even though I was laser-focused on one position, I did look up a couple of other positions that I thought would be a good fit and I even started the application process. But each time, I felt restrained. I never got far into the application process. I kept on hearing the voice in my heart saying, "Stay focused." I was confident that I was being divinely directed (steps being ordered). One thing I didn't want was to be a double-minded man. It was very tough. But I stayed focused, and the good LORD extended mercy and grace to help me de-escalate the situation. I do not encourage you to take my approach unless you are sure that you are sure. Hopefully you will have a longer runway. June to August was a short amount of time, but in my situation that was just how it played out. Sometimes it is all about timing.

RUNWAY LENGTH

A very critical part of my transition was understanding early that I had to transition. Thirty years of service is a hard stopping point for most. I started doing the work early, but not early enough. The transition process began in earnest about 17 months in advance. This was really difficult for me because even though I was intently focusing on being single-minded, I could not stop performing at a high level in my current job and I was in the process of completing my master's degree. Did I say that I did not start early enough? This was extremely difficult but was absolutely necessary.

I decided to dedicate my morning quiet time to flesh out my vision of where I thought I was going. There was a lot of prayer and a lot of journaling that ultimately helped me to figure out what my "next" was. I filled up almost two journals between the time I started preparing and the actual date I began my new career. It was in my journal that I was able to discern needs versus wants. My journal was my first sounding board and allowed me to clarify my thoughts. Because I had a long-ish runway, I did not feel rushed and had plenty of time to seek wise counsel from others. I am confident that if I felt more pressure from not having enough time, I would have made an incorrect decision that would have led to a different path. And not that I would not have been successful on a different path, but I would have likely not found a match between my purpose, passion, and employment. From my perspective, many veterans are seeking a purpose post-military and because this may not be a part of their deliberate decision-making process when transitioning, it leads to changing jobs multiple times. A long runway allows you to vet and re-vet your ideas and thoughts. It allows you and your significant other to have meaningful and thoughtful conversations.

A long runway allows you to create the necessary networks you need to transition to the "new." You need a solid network if you want to transition into "new" at a level higher than entry level. A long runway allows you to obtain the necessary credentialing or at least get a large chunk completed before it is needed for the "new." A long runway allows you to mentally make the necessary adjustments from where you are to the "new." This is something that I wish I had spent more time on, even though I did spend a considerable amount of time focusing on it. But the differences in thought processes as a military member and someone who has not served in the armed services is significant. Whether it is four years or 40 years, the mental conditioning is there. Without intentionally focusing on this you may create chaos, because of wrong expectations. From a common vocabulary and military protocols to basic expectations of individuals in the group, it all takes time to adjust our thinking. The more time we have, the better.

IFES

In aircraft operations, there is an acronym used that automatically gets one's heart rate up—IFE. This technically means in-flight emergency. When this type of situation occurs, many people get activated, inside the aircraft and on the ground. Emergency response functions are dispatched, and everyone is running on high adrenaline. Some examples of in-flight emergencies include, but are not limited to, smoke in the flight deck, medical emergencies while in flight (crew or passenger), landing gear malfunction, loss of cabin pressure, system malfunctions of various types.

But, how does the acronym apply to having "triumphant transitions?" I'm glad you asked. IFEs, in this realm, equate to **inform**, **fuel/follow**, and **empower**.

Inform: First, be informed! If a transition is forecasted, do not wait to get in gear to activate the required buttons and levers. What are those buttons and levers? There are many, but here are some. Know where to find the jobs. Really. It's that simple. I did not know where to find certain jobs, but I knew people working in the industry. I thought, Why not ask them? Get up to speed on trends for document submission and favorable phrasing. Research the positions, companies, and leadership teams for the jobs you will apply for. Then imagine what you could enhance, how your skillset matched the mission, what you bring to the culture of the organization, and whether this could be long- or short-term employment. In some cases, it may be seen as a step backwards, in order to catapult forward.

Scheduling informational interviews is quite beneficial. As I was preparing to end my previous career, I went on several informational interviews. I was pleasantly surprised at how open managers and hiring authorities were to the concept. Two companies in particular could have become employment opportunities very easily. Truthfully, I think about both even today, if I needed to make a change, I would go back to both of them. One executive assisted me with resume preparation considerations if I was to seek opportunities with them.

In fact, he saw a single line on my document and asked me several questions. At the end, he asked if I was actively seeking and would consider changing my timeline. He told me about a position he was looking to fill, and that I would be a great candidate based on the questions from that single line on my resume. Not only that, but the job was also nearby and paid up to $100,000. Talk about temptation! Even after that encounter, this leader expressed his willingness to consider me in the future and would recommend positions based on my experiences.

Another aspect to consider is to inform those that you know, like, and trust about your impending transition. They may produce leads for you. Or may inform you in a way that you can redirect someone else. Planting seeds of goodness in this way may prove to bless you later.

For students, research your schools and then look for people in your network that are alumni from the institution(s) you desire to attend. Seek them out to get advice on your application. They may be able to tell you if you need more volunteer hours or if there is a particular type of volunteer work that garners more favor. They also may be able to provide a recommendation to someone on the inside of the organization that may aid your entrance into the school.

Fuel/Follow: While you are job hunting, be sure to follow links within links. You can potentially build a list of job boards over time. That said, I recommend that you be so familiar with job boards that you know when a new line is added, have a sense of the apply date patterns, and that you develop a natural habit of clicking through sites. That's right. Follow the links and they will fuel your search. Some positions are listed in multiple sites. This may provide exposure to greater opportunities of similar type.

My advice to you is to fuel your passions and follow your purpose and heart. A person is not easily dismayed when they are feeding their purpose and passions, regardless of how hard the situation is. Even during tough times, your resiliency is higher when you are operating in a field that aligns with who you are at the core.

Empower: A simple concept is to let people help you. In my season of transition, there were people that encouraged me along the way. Why? Because they knew and were authorized to talk to me about it. Giving someone permission to provide a different perspective sounds formal, but too many people struggle when others talk to them about sensitive subjects. We must allow people to speak into our lives and future. Empower others to enable you. If you are the type that has helped others, consider that seed for your future harvest. When time comes to reap a measure of return, don't block it.

I feel a need to give a caution. Don't just have people tell you the fun things. You need supportive truth bearers, too. Okay, you need an example. Have you seen those singing contest TV shows? Every person that reached the stage was told by someone that they had what it takes. For real. Now remember the clips of the not so great—okay terrible—singers. Somebody should have redirected those people back to their calling, skill set, or realm of capability. Instead, a friendly person co-signed on it, and now we have clips on the internet forever. A supportive truth bearer had an obligation to intervene. But were they heard or allowed to speak on the issue? Be bold enough to empower people to speak unfiltered truth to you. This will enable you to have greater success and hopefully avoid embarrassment.

REHEARSE WHAT
YOU SEE DAILY

Another tool is to use a dream board or
a vision board. When combined with verbal
affirmations, a dream board becomes a force
multiplier. Jack Canfield said on Twitter:

> Your brain will work tirelessly to achieve
> the statements you give your subconscious
> mind. And when those statements are the
> affirmations and images of your goals, you are
> destined to achieve them! [2]

A vision board is simply taking a poster board
and finding images that speak to you that say
through pictures the vision you see in your head.
The images should elicit deep emotions when
you look at the vision board. You should feel a
sensation come across your body when you spend
time soaking in the images. The images should
give you energy and focus to do more work to
help the vision to come to pass. If you do not have
a rush of emotions, I encourage you to find new
images. Take your time and don't use common

images. Use images that speak to you personally. This may take some time, but once you find them, you won't regret it. Once you establish your collage of pictures that represent your vision, ensure you place it in a location where you can see it routinely.

Visualization is another tool to help defeat double-mindedness, and I believe it is the most powerful. So, what is visualization? Merriam-Webster.com Dictionary indicates that it is a technique involving forming and focusing on positive mental images in order to achieve a particular goal.3 But it goes much deeper than that definition. I can have fanciful visions of one day living a certain lifestyle or having a level of health and never achieve it. Visualization requires intentionally focusing to create a very vivid mental picture and then inserting yourself into the picture as if you already had what you desire.

The type of visualization I am talking about is seeing yourself in the room wearing the clothes and shoes to be in the role you desire. You should be able to visualize the conversations you might have. You should be able to visualize the people with whom you would be interacting. You should be able to insert yourself into the movie in your mind as if you were a stunt-double, but in reality, you are the star. You have to see it, before you can see it.

WHAT YOU ARE GOOD AT VS.
WHAT YOU ARE CALLED TO DO

What are you good at? What comes naturally for you? Some wonder if these things are what they are supposed to do or be for the remainder of their lives. It may very well be. But it likely isn't.

Just like our personalities, we are shaped over time, likely over a lifetime. Our experiences open us up to new concepts, skills, and desires. At various stages of life, if one did a career assessment, there may be differing outcomes. But I would challenge you to see if there is a common thread across all portions of your life.

Your work, social, spiritual, and introspective lives are all connected. If you can discover what links are connected, you may identify your gifts and callings. Some may classify it as your purpose.

I heard a concept some years ago that indicated that we should not expect to get all we need in life from a single source. Like investment principles, have a diversified portfolio, except for your income sources. The diversity should not be looked at as a hazard.

Think back to your teenage days. What was your first job? Did you grow and learn from that experience? Have you used any of that knowledge since then? What about your second job? Same drill… It is compounding in nature, very much the same as compound interest. In fact, it is the exact same process and result.

My encouragement is this, look at the progression that you have had, and do not be afraid to add to it. Even when the path is not a seemingly linear route. Imagine this, a young lady volunteered as a teenager in her family friend's business. She worked on filing and scheduling activities. Then she gets a job in a grocery store as a stocker and bagger. She attends college but doesn't finish. Her degree plan was business related. Then she worked a few administrative jobs while going to night school to finish her degree. Upon finishing her degree, she sought a management position.

In her preparation, it would be wise for her to

account for the knowledge and skill progression over the last 10 years. This could easily reach back to volunteer time as a teen. She should evaluate the common themes of experiences. Do the puzzle pieces start forming a picture?

FISHING VS. HUNTING

I have a friend and mentor named Abie, who is a corporate recruiter. He served in that role in the Air Force and continues in the corporate world. Some years ago, I reached out to him about a team member who was leaving uniformed service soon. I was hoping to discover some opportunities for my teammate. Then I was asked a crucial question, "What does he want to do?" I mentioned the skills he had and where I noticed strengths. Again I got the question, "What does he want to do?" So, I went back to pose the question. Unexpectedly, I got a broad, unfocused answer. So, I thought it best not to be the middleman, and directly connect the two of them. They had a few conversations and eventually my friend called me. His words will stick with me for years to come, "Your guy is fishing. He needs to become a hunter."

I pondered this statement for a while, and then I doubled back to get more clarity. On the surface, I understood that he needed to really focus and not be scattered. After talking with Abie, he caused me to evaluate the processes and actions that go along with fishing and hunting. There really is a difference in approach.

Fishing involves having equipment, bait, lures, tackle box, net, bucket, or container. As a simple explanation, an angler doing shoreline fishing may use a fishing rod, hook, worm, and a bobber. She would cast out into the lake, let the weight of the worm slowly sink to the length of the line while the bobber rests on the top of the water. The work and benefit opportunity happens under the water, out of the sight of the angler. Literally in the blind in most cases. When she gets a bite, she doesn't know what is on the hook until she gets it close enough to the surface. This angler may know which fish is desired, or what is in the lake, but it comes down to hoping to be in the right place, at the right time. Anticipating that something under the water will see, smell, or notice the bait. Did you notice the word I used? Hope.

Hunting, on the other hand, is different all together. The hunter goes out to acquire a specific target. The patterns and places of the prey are studied, and the hunter is able to go directly to the most optimal location at the best-known time, based on the information that is available. A skillful hunter will be aware of the associated rules and regulations, sizes, gender differences, seasons of authorization, prohibited actions. He knows when to wait and when to engage.

Think about that. When to wait and when to engage. One could be seeking a certain animal. If anything else walks by that could be food it is allowed to walk by unimpeded. If the right type is within range, but the wrong size, age or gender, the hunter may gain sight alignment, but not pull the trigger. In fact, the animal may be watched, in the effort to discover if there is an appropriate target nearby or connected to the one you don't want. Firing at the wrong target may scare off the one you really want. This is a detrimental distraction.

Take it deeper. In the context of job seeking or starting a business, would you rather be separated from and blind to the activities surrounding your goal, or is it better to study, discover patterns, be in the right place at the most opportune times, and see the activities surrounding your position? Fishing for a job is throwing applications into the lake of whatever is out there, being scattered in your focus, hoping for one thing but not being able to see if it is near or nibbling. Conversely, job hunting is much narrower in scope. The process is not fixed on blind hope or casting in various directions wondering what or who will see, notice, or bite your bait.

You may know the type of work you want to find but may not be focused on a particular company, and that is fine. On the other hand, you may desire to get into a particular company, with a targeted long-term plan within that system. There is nothing wrong with that logic. But if the approach is to throw everything against the wall and see what sticks, you can get a job. But will you be fulfilled or satisfied? A way to avoid what may be seen as desperation is to properly plan and engage well in advance of need. This includes widening your sphere of influence and network.

When others are willing to contribute to your journey, you should have a clear vision of what you are going for. You should have the 45 to 90 second elevator speech, plus the relevant background that leads you this way or supports the value you bring. Always have a readiness to share at the next level the purpose and the real 'why.' For some, this will be very personal, and that is okay. If an interviewer can discern your passion or purpose, it may compensate, cover, or offset a perceived shortfall.

4.

PRESS PAST THE PAST

WHAT GOT YOU HERE
WON'T GET YOU THERE

Play by the rules of the game that you are in.
This is a concept that developed as a result of
an exchange I had with a dear friend. I received
notification of a promotion. Unfortunately, he
was not selected in the same cycle. We met to
talk through our approaches to occupational
preparation and spiritual discipline, because
he was a leader at work and at church. Our
promotion system included a knowledge test,
so I asked him to bring his study material for
work and his Bible. He was nervous, not knowing
my intentions, as our job was very strict about
prohibiting group study sessions. We didn't open
either set of materials. I merely inquired about his
study habits for work and church and pointed out
how they were different. He knew his job, but he
really knew the faith principles he lived by. It was
obvious that he spent a greater amount of time
in one of the two areas. We also discussed the
differences between reading and studying.

Then, I shifted the discussion. I asked him to name a sport with a goalie. His first answer was soccer; his second response was hockey. These are the two most common answers that I get, in fact, I usually get them in that order. Every now and then someone will say lacrosse. I invited him to imagine a scenario where I was a soccer goalie. I'm not just a soccer goalie, I'm a good soccer goalie! I have my fancy shirt on, my good gloves, my cleats and plenty of confidence. If anybody runs into me, they get a penalty. There are others on the team who protect me. Anytime someone kicks the ball towards my goal I am all over it! Hardly anything gets by me.

One day, I get the idea to transfer from soccer to the hockey rink. My level of competence and confidence allows me to go in with a high expectation that I will do well in hockey. The only thing is, I don't plan to make any changes. Everything that got me to where I am regarding soccer should be able to hold me in the rink, right?

So here I am, fancy shirt, nice gloves, cleats, and if anybody runs into me, they get a penalty. I got this. The cleats and ice are not a match as it is, but as soon as somebody slaps the puck towards the goal that I'm defending, I am sure to take a trip to the hospital.

My error in this could be considered a halo bias or something similar. Because I was good in one sport, based on a position, I thought I would be able to hold the same position in another sport without making any changes. My error? I did not play by the rules of the game that I was in.

I did not change the equipment, adjust my logic, or even implement any additional safety measures.

When one is transitioning or looking for advancement, it is unrealistic to expect that no adjustments would be needed. One's previous successes do not automatically slingshot them into future opportunities. You have to play by the rules of the game that you are in. No exceptions.

I know people that retired from the military. Some of them assumed that they would easily get a big leadership job, or they were perfectly suited for a Human Resources Director position. The error was they expected it and did not prepare for it.

They kept their military uniform (fancy shirt) on their LinkedIn profile. They spoke military jargon and acronyms (gloves). Some wanted things at the fast pace they once kept (cleats on the ice rink). When problems come their way, they revert to the old way of responding. Hockey pucks are smaller and travel much faster than a soccer ball. They are harder to see at times. People can get hurt quickly.

Even changing companies within the same field comes with adjustments. The employers will have different expectations that will take some time to get used to. It doesn't matter what worked well in your last job, when you are new and unknown. There may be an institutional strategy that prevents the other method or approach from implementation in the new setting. But you don't know that yet, so be careful not to become the newest problem in the organization.

When preparing to enter a new field or company, we must be diligent to discover the nuances of difference and choose to adjust or not. By all means, avoid being blind to the truth of the situation. Unrealistic expectations often produce disappointment. If you can't change them, simply play by the rules of the game you are in.

Much thought must be given to this area well in advance of the transition. Why? The longer you were in your previous career, the more implicit biases you will have, whether you admit it or not. You have very diligently learned the rules of the game and excelled. This can cause blind spots because you can operate on autopilot and not even realize that you are in autopilot mode. This shows up in jargon, communication style and frequency, handling of staff, expected customs and courtesies. There are so many little nuances that get in the way of successful transitions.

You must be intentional to be a continual learner and go "back to school" prior to, during, and after the transition. What got you here, won't get you there. You must be a voracious consumer of information on a quest to attain knowledge about where you want to go. Your level of effort must match and even exceed the effort you put in from your previous career. Don't let the halo effect fool you into believing that you are really that good. If you choose to put in that same level of effort, you know the odds are in your favor that you may have the level of success you desire.

Your track record shows it. You transitioned as a Chief Master Sergeant, Sergeant Major, or Master Chief which is the top 1% of the enlisted force. How many people make it to the top 1% of anything? You transitioned as a successful leader or manager who led a team who were the "boots on the ground" in a multi-million-dollar business merger. You completed four years of honorable service to your nation. How many people successfully complete a minimum of four years of service and transition with an honorable discharge? Less than .5% of the American population. You successfully completed your undergraduate degree. My point is, if you were successful in your previous role, the same success is within your reach as you transition. You just need to put in the same amount of effort. In fact, it is imperative that you put in the same level of effort to learn the new requirements to be successful as defined by the new environment and take nothing for granted. You have to go hard!

REARVIEW MIRRORS

A major component of a successful transition is letting go of the past. I often tell people there is a reason why the windshield is much bigger than the rearview mirror. The windshield is designed to be so big so you can see where you are going and avoid obstacles. If we find ourselves looking in the rearview mirror too much, one of two things will happen: (1) We will crash, (2) We will miss our exit (opportunity). Something else of note is the name windshield. The glass is shielding you from the wind. What causes the wind? The vehicle is in motion going somewhere. The car and driver have a destination to get to. The motion to get to the destination requires one to be shielded from the wind. Looking backwards into the past where we came from does not require any motion, and therefore, a windshield is not required.

After serving for four, ten, twenty, or forty years, the uniform starts to become a part of you, whether you see it or not. For some of us it becomes a bigger part than others, which will make the transition from the military more tough. For someone who has been in sales for 15-20 years or been an educator for 30 years, the transition to something new will be tough. You poured your blood, sweat, and tears into getting really good at your craft and becoming a subject matter expert. You have gained a certain level of credibility with your bosses, peers, and subordinates because of your skill sets.

Your work has inevitably become, to some degree, a part of you. If you think that you can be doing something for a number of years and the next day you can flip a switch and forget all of the previous career, you are in for a surprise. If you were able to do this, you are a part of a unique group. I served in the military for 30 years starting at the rank of E-1. There were lots of victories and losses over those 30 years. Numerous highs and lows and experiences that molded me into a responsible adult. Opportunities that gave me the chance to reach self-actualization. My children grew up in military surroundings and understood military jargon. There was no way I could just flip a switch and forget all of that.

Yet, I could not afford to drag all of that with me into my future. If we continue to compare the present to the past, we will never be satisfied. The present has to be viewed and evaluated in the context of the present, and not in the context of the past. Otherwise, we will make decisions that won't be precise. I think looking back to the past is a key reason why many veterans change jobs multiple times after retirement. They are looking at their current job or career through the lenses of their military career. This is no different for an educator or an engineer, or a transitioning senior. We attempt to scratch an itch in the same manner that we did previously, despite the fact we have a different tool.

For example, what I loved about the military was "service." I was serving a cause greater than me, and therefore, I was willing to make sacrifices. When I retired, I had to keep in mind that there was no way I was going to scratch that itch in the same way as I previously did in the military. While in uniform, I made a conscious decision that, if necessary, I would write a check with my life to preserve and protect the ideal of "We hold these truths to be self-evident, that all men are created equal, that they are endowed by their Creator with certain unalienable Rights, that among these are Life, Liberty and the pursuit of Happiness. That to secure these rights, Governments are instituted among Men."4 When I retired, I had to find a new way to scratch my itch for service and not compare everything I did through the lens of military service. If I did that, nothing would live up to the experience. I would likely be frustrated and unhappy and this might cause me to jump from job to job as I looked in the rearview mirror, all the while missing new exits that could give me what I desired in a new way and lead to new desirable experiences.

For a high school student, it might be that you were the captain of your team and very popular. Perhaps everyone sought you out, but now, as a freshman on a new campus, you get swallowed up and lost in the crowd. Whatever your situation is, you look forward, otherwise, may get off of the best path towards your future.

Additionally, as I transitioned, I had to understand that once I retired, the rank and respect I had attained would not necessarily translate at a rate of one-to-one. If I would have been looking in the rearview mirror, I would have expected the customs and courtesies of my former rank, even though I was not in a uniform. For me, I had grown accustomed to having a seat at the table and my voice being valid and relevant in many areas despite the fact I was not an expert in the subject matter. I appreciate that I was able to add value to a conversation as an "outsider." I had to come to grips that this may not be the case going forward. I will admit, this mental shift did not happen overnight.

For you it might be having perks like a private elevator or always flying first class. Regardless of the career, there are always perks, privileges, systems and courtesies. Truth-in-lending, I have been retired at this point for almost four years, and I am still working on this. It has been a struggle and I have had to work very intentionally to not get tripped up by this. I am a fast learner and can put multiple various disparate pieces of random information together in ways that can lead to better outcomes. But even today, everyone I interact with is not open to my input. I have to constantly remind myself it is not a right to be at the table and be heard in the same way I was previously heard.

Most of the time, externally I breathe through my nose (exhale) and smile, but there are still times I catch myself saying, "If I was at base X, they would have listened and considered my input." But thank GOD, I have developed the skill to break the "rearview mirror thought" and redirect my mind and refocus on the windshield. Otherwise, I might sabotage my present and future, by staying locked on the past, which can never be revisited. If I compare my present relationships (professional and personal) to my past relationships, I would be ineffective in the world that I currently operate in and find myself in a constant state of flux. My job is not to compare the past with the present. My job is to understand the present in the context of the present, use applicable tools from the past as a baseline, identify skill gaps and figure out how to be effective in the present by looking forward toward the future (keep the end in mind from the beginning).

Why does looking forward toward the future help me to be effective? Where there is no vision, there is no restraint. Vision (looking forward through the windshield) gives me a left and right boundary. Vision forces me to make choices to get to where I desire to be. Even if what I am currently doing is not what I want to do long-term, vision helps me to make more effective non-self-sabotaging short-term decisions that will empower my long-term goals and objectives. What I have observed is that a lot of people make short-term decisions because they are looking in the rearview mirror and self-sabotaging their futures. Now when I say "self-sabotage" that does not mean they don't lead productive lives. What I mean is, they don't posture themselves to self-actualize after the transition. They don't posture themselves to have a similar level of fulfillment and satisfaction. Rearview mirror thinking makes it difficult to get lost in the hunt of the "pursuit." What tends to happen is they have Monday Blues and Friday Resurrections as the weekend approaches, and they get furloughed for two days.

HANDCUFFS

- William Shakespeare [5]

It was alluded to in the previous section, but we will deal with it more directly here. We covered rearview mirrors, but now we will address fear. From my perspective fear is the #1 handcuff. President John F. Kennedy said, "There are fears and costs to a program of action, but they are far less than the long-range risks and costs of comfortable inaction."6 For clarity's sake let's define "handcuffs." The use of the word here is to connotate a paralyzing thought or series of thoughts that prevent a person from taking an action(s) that are in their long-term best interests.

The fear of the unknown. It has trapped many people in the past and will undoubtedly trap many people in the future. Can I do that? Am I good enough? Am I smart enough to do that? Am I too old? Am I old enough? What if I try and fail? What will people think? Will my old colleagues ridicule me? The potential questions go on and on and each successive question seems to exponentially increase the strength of the handcuffs. It is as if they build on one another until eventually, they evolve from handcuffs to an actual cage. We must also be ever so mindful of the negative impact of handcuffs. It will be addressed later, but you must remove "fire fighters" from your circle. It is a critically important component.

As much as we may not want to admit, even the person who is an extremely high performing individual wrestles with these thoughts. And it is not abnormal for the thoughts to come. We should, in fact, expect them to come. The problem is not that they come, but the problem arises when we allow them to come and to take up residence in our minds (renting space). This is the beginning stages of the development of handcuffs. When we expect that negative thoughts will try to creep in, we can better recognize when they come and be prepared to deal with them.

If we fail to know or acknowledge, they will

try to creep in. It is as if they are camouflaged or "cloaked" in broad daylight. They are right in front of our eyes, but we take no notice of them as they begin to plant their seeds and allow the seeds to germinate in our minds. When this happens, by the time we realize the enemy has creeped into our camp the seeds have germinated, sprouted, and have a well-established plant system (root, stem, and leaves). The longer we allow the fearful thought to stay in the soil of our mind, the more paralyzing it becomes as the roots dig in deeper and its stem system matures and starts to bear fruit. The fruit it bears are the handcuffs. Examples of the fruit are failing to apply for the position you know you are qualified for. Not pursuing and completing the certificate you need to be competitive for a position. Settling for a job that you don't really want.

The challenge is that the fear-based thoughts appear so powerful. I remember as I was about two years out from my mandatory transition timeline of 30 years of service. I started to have conversations with myself and my Maker about what "next" would look like. As my vision and purpose started to emerge, the position of a Chief Operating Officer emerged in my heart. And when I just embraced the moment in its pure form, I began to really feel excitement coursing through my veins. The more I thought about it the more excited I became. But then right on cue the paralyzing thoughts (handcuffs) showed up. Do you know that you are a Chief and not an officer? Why do you think you could do that? Do you have the education to do that? Could you actually succeed at doing that? Why would they want to hire someone who was enlisted into that role? Why would they want to hire you into that role?

The number of negative thoughts I had to battle were relentless. And this was further exacerbated by the fact that when I had the courage to mention what I had in my heart, several of my peers reinforced the negative thought of "Chiefs don't do that." I had to fight for what I now know was the vision GOD implanted in my heart. I used to be upset with my peers during my transition when they were not supportive. But in hindsight, the bottom line is that they did not say what they said with the sole purpose of raining on my parade. They saw themselves the same way and so their words reflected that. So, one thing of note, as you go through your transition, don't take it personal when people close to you are not supportive. It's not necessarily how they see you. It could be how they see themselves.

This means that during your transition, you and you are alone are responsible for tending to the "garden of your mind." You have to pull weeds daily and often multiple times in a day and on occasion, multiple times in an hour to ensure your crop is not overtaken by the weeds. Weeds rob the "crop" of the vital nutrients it needs to provide you a long-term harvest. Be intentional to not only pull weeds but also to water and fertilize the seeds you desire to see grow to produce the harvest you desire to see. One component of this, which will be discussed later, is having "fire lighters" in your circle. I would highly suggest you have at least two in your circle, because a three-strand cord is not easily broken. And, of course, the more you have the better off you are.

WRONG EXPECTATIONS

When I retired in June of 2017, I continued to live on base for the next three months until my official retirement as I sought employment in the local community and a new place to live. This meant that every day when I walked out of my house nothing had changed other than I did not wear my uniform. I saw the same people and smelled the same jet fuel. Little did I know that this was a trap for me to remain stuck mentally, meaning, even though I had retired and was no longer doing the job, in my mind there was the potential to remain stuck and not move forward. People still called me "Chief" and gave me the same respect and adoration that they had previously. And whether I wanted to admit it or not, I enjoyed the respect that I had earned from them and the adoration they chose to give.

In transition, we must be keenly aware of our desire to be respected and adored. And if you have attained any level of success with a group of people, through hard work, sweat and tears, you, too, have a measure of respect and adoration. I do not feel this is necessarily a bad thing, as long as it is not out of balance. In most cases, the respect rightfully deserved because you have made sacrifices and poured into your teams as you grew them and with them.

Yet we all must remember that this success did not happen overnight. It took time to garner the expertise and earn the respect of those we led and worked for and with. As we transition, we need to be careful not to expect the same level of respect and adoration. If we continue to do the things that we did previously it will come in time.

I remember when I first transitioned, over the first two and a half years I experienced a lot of frustrations because people did not seek my input in areas outside of where they thought I had expertise. In the military across all branches to attain the level of Chief Master Sergeant, Sergeant Major, or Master Chief, is no small feat. Once at that level, because of the respect for what it takes to be promoted to that rank, people seek out your input in a wide variety of areas because you are a trusted and seasoned sounding board.

I did not realize it at first, but this frustrated me deep down inside and it began to swell and eventually made it to the surface. At the time I was working with an executive coach, and we caught it before it caused me to self-sabotage. The bottom line was that most of the people I worked with and for had no clue as to what it took to become a Chief and never would. So, I just needed to get over it. I needed to just continue to grind and take care of my people like I did to become a Chief. Period dot. The conversation I had with myself was, So what, son? Suck it up buttercup and keep it moving. Show them who you are.

While most did not understand what it took to reach the rank nor be selected for the jobs I held, there was some translation. Because of my former boss, who was well respected in the local community, I was respected. My boss spoke highly of me in many rooms in the community when I was not present. As a result, there were many people who thought about me when the position I am in now opened up.

Several key local community members knew

that I was a key part of the leadership team at the base that oversaw a workforce of 8,000 and an installation that took care of 31,000 family members and retirees. They understood and respected what it took to lead at that level, which I greatly appreciated. This got my foot in the door. There were also some other key advocates who really understood this and worked hard to try and retain me in their community. And although this was and is still flattering, it also was a huge push for me to work hard and not let them down. I respected and appreciated their advocacy.

In my transition, I had another conversation. This one was with my uniform. Yes, my uniform. Again, I served for 30 years, so my uniform had become a part of me to a certain degree. Then the rank I held meant a lot to me and had become a part of me to a degree (I will always be a Chief). As stated previously, I was still on base too. I had three months to secure employment and hopefully a new career and move off base. I did not have time to be stuck looking in the rearview mirror.

I would see people and they would still seek
out my advice on things pertaining to the military
and their careers. I was positioned to very easily
pay lip service to moving forward while being
stuck in the past. I had a wife and three kids at
home, so I had to be focused. One day my wife
and kids left the house to do something, and I
had a conversation with my uniform. I hung it up
on the door and I squared off with it. It took me
a minute to gather myself, but I composed myself
and began. It went something like this:

Hello uniform.
I need for you to know that you are not me and
I am not you. I wore you for 30 years. I served
my nation for 30 years and I served well. But
I am not you and you are not me. My name is
Christopher Hope McKinney. I wore the title of
Chief Master Sergeant, and I was very proud to
be selected to serve in that capacity. But I am
not you and you are not me. I say again, I am
not you and you are not me. My name is Chris,
and you are something I did for a period of
time in my life. I served my country well but
that is not the full definition of who I am. You

are not me and I am not you! I know whose I am and who I am. I am not you! You are not me! I appreciate the experiences we had together, but I am going to hang you up now and move on. I will use many of the experiences I gained, but I am going to move forward.

I had tears streaming down my face as I had the conversation, but it was a conversation I had to have in order to move forward.

5.

GET
AFTER
THE
GAPS

**"WE CANNOT BECOME WHAT WE NEED
BY REMAINING WHAT WE ARE."**

- Max De Pree

DO YOU KNOW YOUR GAPS?

Getting after the gaps to help you transition successfully requires intentionality and humility. We must be able to accurately assess where we are and what we need to do to get to where we want to be. It also requires that we do our homework to have a clear understanding of what is required to be successful in the new pursuit. Are there educational requirements? Are certificates required? Do I need a certain amount of experience doing something that is not translatable out of my resume? How can I improve my industry vocabulary? Should I consider obtaining a new wardrobe? Does this require me to work on my public speaking? Do I need to work on my writing skills? Do I need to improve my people skills? Are there people that I need to meet?

The last one is one where I struggled when coming out of the military and trying to meet people (networking for the sake of trying to get something). It was very uncomfortable, as I felt like I was doing something shady. In my head initially, it felt like I was using people. And the bottom line is that I was to a degree using people because I approached it the wrong way. I needed to meet people so they could get to know me and get a better feel for who I was and what I brought to the table. I did not need to meet people solely for the sake of what they could do for me. I needed them to be able to see things the resume could not convey. I needed to connect. Also, what I had to realize was that it was not a one-way transaction. As I sought to meet people to network, the fact was that whomever I started a new career with was going to get a great deal. I was going to bring all my gifts and talents the good LORD had blessed me with along with 30 years of "the mission cannot and will not fail" attitude. Having me on the team had a huge upside for the potential employer. So, whoever helped connect me, their credibility would be bolstered, guaranteed!

So, I will tell you in my final 18 months in the toughest and busiest job of my life. I knew I needed to complete my graduate degree to have a fighting shot. This meant early days and late nights while still trying to maintain some semblance of a family life with my wife and three kids at home. It was not easy and there were many times I wanted to quit, like when I was in the middle of a statistics class. (I hate statistics.) I was not comprehending the content and the deadline to submit a major paper was approaching. I wanted to scream! But because I had a definiteness of purpose (single-minded) and I knew this was a no-compromise gap, I did what I had to do. I don't know how many YouTube videos I watched to get a better understanding of the content to pass the class with a B-.

All of that "pain" was necessary for me to close the gaps. (Did I mention having a long runway is helpful?) It was not fun and as previously stated, I wanted to quit multiple times, but I hung in there because I had a vision. You have to be committed to closing the gaps

DO AN ANALYSIS

Author Kilroy J. Oldster wrote, "If a person wishes to engender self-improvement, they must eschew conventional norms and seek an authentic conversation with the self. I need to acknowledge all my ugly warts..."7 After having attained a certain level of success, this may be difficult and even painful for us to execute. As we climb higher and attain more success, people will tend to overlook the minor flaws we have and the mistakes we make as long as they don't escalate or become a detriment. This means if we do not have people in our circle who give us honest feedback, we may resist the need to evaluate all of the tiny pimples and imperfections that are not easily seen when we zoom out to the 1X level but are plainly visible at the 10X zoom level. We must exercise emotional intelligence and press past the pain of the obvious if we want to see a similar level of success in our new endeavors.

What are my strengths? What are my weaknesses? Which of my weak areas are needed in the new career? What do I need to improve to become an "impact player" in my new endeavor? There are plenty of other questions to ask, so the question is how do I get the answers?

GET OUTSIDE INPUT

There are a few different ways to approach it. There is the honest feedback from your significant other. They may not be versed in your field but can offer key input. I know sometimes their input can be painful to receive because they more than anyone see us at our best and our worst. There is no veneer when it comes to how we appear to them.

Next you can seek feedback from trusted high performers in your current field. What do they see as your strengths and weaknesses? Where do they think you can improve? You can also seek feedback from people in the field you desire to transition. When I was transitioning, I sat down with several people who although they did not know my skill sets fully, there was some valuable insight they provided with regards to skills I would need in the new endeavor.

And then there are executive coaches. In the military, I had the privilege to attend a class facilitated by an executive coach and they gave us materials to help with the evaluation. I have been working with an executive coach for the past three years and I cannot express the value of this service. The inquiries, prompting, and probing have helped me to continue to self-evaluate and grow. Their input also can affirm when we are on the right track, when no one else sees the bigger picture. Whatever you do, you must conduct an analysis.

DEVELOP A DELIBERATE PLAN

Stephen Keague is quoted saying, "Proper planning and preparation prevents poor performance." Once the gaps are identified, now it is time to get to work. The more time you have until your planned transition (long runway) the better. Motivational speaker Brian Tracy stated, "A clear vision, backed by definite plans, gives you a tremendous feeling of confidence and personal power." The longer your runway, the clearer your vision will be and the more confidence you will have in your transition. You may need to take a class or two to brush up on the latest concepts in the field. You may need to get a certificate. You may need to go back to school to get an additional degree. You may need to learn a new language. Whatever the gaps are, be sure to give yourself as much time as possible to prepare.

Brian Tracy also stated, "Every minute you spend in planning saves 10 minutes in execution; this gives you a 1,000 percent return on energy!" In my transition on July 29, 2017, I became very clear about what my next move was going to be. I spent from July 29th until my first interview on September 6, 2017, doing my homework to prepare for my next career. And mind you, I did not get notified that I had been selected for an interview until August 29, 2017. I read everything I could find about the organization. I even went to their building to pick up a copy of some of their documents. I read and re-read their information as if I were preparing to execute a military mission. I studied. I evaluated it. I looked at how my strengths played into their mission. I looked at what I needed to do to get better in my weak areas, so when they asked me about my weakness, I spoke to them with confidence. On October 5, 2017, I had an in-person interview and I received notice on October 9, 2017, that I had been selected for the position.

GET AFTER IT CONSISTENTLY

In the book, "Training Camp" by Jon Gordon there is a chapter called "Telescope" and in it he highlights three principles: (1) The best know what they truly want. Meaning they narrow their focus and concentrate on what they truly want; (2) The best want it more. There is one statement in the book that says, "The best don't simply think about their desire for greatness, they act on it. They have a high capacity for work"; (3) The best are always striving to get better.[8]

If you were successful in your previous endeavors, I am confident you applied these principles to get where you arrived. I am also convinced that you did this on a consistent basis that exceeded your peers, because you were driven. You must apply the same drive and fervor in getting after your gaps. If you do, I expect that you may have the same, if not greater, level of success as previously experienced.

You are likely to also see that because you applied these principles previously to become successful, there is a "compound interest" effect when you apply the principles again. What is the compound interest effect? Very simply put, by investing $400 a month at a 5% return at the end of 12 months I do not merely have $4,800. I will have $5,332.01. Not that spectacular, I get it. But let's look at what happens over 30 years. Instead of having $144,000 ($400 X 12 weeks X 30 years), you would have $334,690.55 which is a significant difference.

But what does compound interest have to do with you and getting after it consistently? Glad you asked. Because you have used the three principles above for a number of years in your pursuit of excellence you now are poised to see explosive growth. It is not new to you. You are not developing muscle memory to get good and consistent at "the process." You already have muscle memory for "the process," and therefore, in most cases it will not take as long for you to get up to speed in areas where you are weak, in your effort to transition. You have got this. So get after it, consistently!

REEVALUATE AND REASSESS

**"PLANS ARE OF LITTLE IMPORTANCE,
BUT PLANNING IS ESSENTIAL."**

-Winston Churchill

To ensure you are staying on track with your goals you have to stop and assess from time to time. Depending on how long your runway is, you may have to assess more frequently to ensure you land precisely where you desire. What do we mean by this? Are you pursuing the right educational goals? As you network and talk to more people in the sector you desire to transition to, you may obtain additional information that may cause you to shift your focus in education. Are you taking classes at the speed necessary to obtain the credentials necessary for the transition? Are you taking the necessary classes in the right order?

You may need to double up and take two classes per semester while working fulltime as a mom or dad or outside of the home, because certain things are required to get into certain doors (just a reminder that a longer runway is better). You may also find out that you need to reevaluate the priority of your credentialing plan if you have to obtain multiple certificates. Some are important and some are of the utmost importance. The point is, you need to stop and assess to ensure you can meet your goals. Put a reminder on your calendar to hold yourself accountable.

SIDEBAR #1:
ACCOUNTABILITY THROUGH YOUR CALENDAR

As HH and I embarked on writing this book, in the beginning I was not very consistent. I knew this had to change if I were going to hold up my end of the deal. In my quiet time in the cool of the day, I decided to put one and a half hours on my calendar Monday-Saturday to dedicate to writing. For the first month, I followed it to a "T." Then in month two, things got crazy at work, and I stopped protecting that time to write.

You know how it goes, once you fall off the wagon, it is easy to stay on the ground and that is exactly what happened for six weeks. I wrote some, but not consistently. But what was happening was I was still seeing the book writing time pop up on my calendar and in reminders daily. Also, people who had access to my calendar would periodically ask me about how the book was coming. All of this prompted me to get back on the wagon. What's the point? Even if you don't follow your plan exactly, by putting it on your calendar repetitively you have a greater shot at meeting your goal(s). There is a measure of accountability.

Also, if the baby is ugly, don't sweat it! It's okay. You have to start somewhere. The mighty Oak Tree doesn't start off as a majestic tree. It starts off as a quite unattractive and unassuming acorn. Cut yourself some slack, just get after the gaps!

MIND THE GAPS & MINE THE GAPS

People, not time, stand still. Trees, not humans, produce while being still. What do I want to be when I grow up? What do I want to do next? What is within reach or desired? How do I get there?

All of these are questions we have asked ourselves and others. It's the typical goal setting and go-getting methodology. We are familiar with the concept but are horrible at applying it in our lives. Do we think we can just hope things into existence? Hope is not a plan, and a plan is not action. If you only sit on the seat of "do nothing," disappointment will visit your house. If you hope for a promotion and perform less than average, or hope for all A's and fail to study, you might be setting yourself up for disappointment.

Have you ever heard that hope deferred makes the heart sick? It's true. Have you seen a person that had a deep desire for something for a very long time? So much that it almost consumes them? If the person was not proactive, and expected everything to magically fall into place, they could blindly blame others for not recognizing them.

Think about this; I want a garden in my yard. I identify the perfect spot, lay it out in my mind and even go so far as to discuss it with loved ones. At some point I visit the local nursery and toss my ideas around with the staff. I learn the impacts of the seasons and weather, and all that is relevant. Then I go back to the house and wait. I extend my faith and make plenty of prayers too! And each week, I look in the place where my garden belongs, and...nothing. Who's at fault? My family? The nursery workers? The home builder? Did GOD not hear my prayers? Faith without corresponding actions is just hope. Or a dream.

But wait. Dreams are not just for the bedroom! They are for the living room and the board room. The way you plan, coordinate and track progress at work is what you should be doing regarding personal ambitions. You have got to plan your work and then work your plan. Institute milestones and accountability, even if you are the only person on the team.

Here's what happened to me...

February 2018: First mention of comparison of responsibilities in a casual conversation.

May 2018: First verbal, in a public setting, use of the job as a future potential. I was provided a web link to help me 'find those jobs.' I had a close friend that started working for the local government in 2017, so I inquired about his job and how he liked it. From that point forward the intrigue gradually increased. In fact, my friend started what may be categorized as accountable encouragement. He perceived that this could be a viable option for my next career.

August 2018: First mentoring session with a seasoned professional, 33 years of experience, because interest dramatically increased. An evaluation of relative skills and experiences, educational needs, certification and continuing exposure to functional logic, associations and conferences were some of the major topics discussed. I was seeking a reality check on my viability to pursue this line of work. The guidance from this conversation fueled the decision to move towards this type of employment.

September 2018: As a follow up action to the conversation in August, I enrolled in and started another degree plan in September. Beyond that, my outreach to people in the industry from various locations around the U.S. increased, through the use of LinkedIn. One of the seemingly random profile reviews produced, opportunity to speak with a city manager in another state.

Utilizing LinkedIn purely as a professional networking site has been a tremendous blessing! I established a weekly routine to update my online presence, review job advertisements, formulate questions for others, watch videos or listen to podcasts associated with the profession and begin preparation for interviews. The connection with a Kentucky City Manager was an attempt by me to increase my confidence, by seeing someone that was in the military that is doing what I want to do.

Within minutes of reaching out to this person, he not only accepted the connection electronically, but he also provided an offer to talk, and gave me a phone number to call. We discussed how his transition went and he gave me great encouragement. Over the next month or so, someone told me I should look this person up, which reinforced the good feelings that had already developed.

Along the same timeline, I sought out an association that was identified in August. The leader that I encountered was very helpful and told me about a live online webinar that was available for me to call into. He advised that I think about questions in advance, the topic, veterans in local government.

November 2018: Who could have planned this? The pre-talk about the webinar, the Kentucky manager discussion, the mentorship from the Town next door. When I discovered the date for the webinar it literally was during the time my flight to Ohio was in the air. When I asked the association leader if it would be recorded, he said yes and asked me for the list of questions I prepared. Not only that, but he was also the moderator for the webinar. And the City Manager from Kentucky was a guest speaker for the event! What? When

I received the link to the recording (early access), the moderator asked some of my questions.

My next step was to inquire of the association to find out how I could become a member. When I opened my email, it contained a partially filled out application. My response: take my money!

The next goal that was set included having a resume and cover letter ready for prime time by August of 2019, one year in advance of my anticipated end of contract. When that goal was established, it invited distractions. Friends, colleagues, and senior leaders started encouraging me and enticing me to prepare for opportunities within their organizations and industries. Seriously, I was approached at various dinners, emailed, called, invited to special meetings. In all of this, I started considering the relationships and the value these professionals placed on me.

Beyond that, I fielded a few informational interviews that gave me some hope. It got so far as to me signing up for a self-paced training program for a company. Oops, that's not part of the plan. But it felt good to be welcomed and wanted. While talking to a close friend and mentor, he heard some of my comments and pulled the emergency brake on me. He reminded me of my goal and my perception of what I was supposed to do.

So, I informed company 'A' and company 'B' of my long-term intent. Oddly enough, they were not shaken. Company 'A' asked me for my transition timeline, then said for me to reach back out in January or February 2020, when it would be time to solidify my intent. Company 'B' understood and stated that the door was always open. They then set me up to talk with another employee so that I could hear more of their testimony.

My friend's answer when I told him about it, "That's a distraction!" Focus, set, and maintain a single focus. Let your eye be single is a phrase we both are familiar with. But it is important to note the appeal to the attention I was getting. It was kind of like being a smitten teenager. You know, but he likes me, she keeps giving me attention, they know me and would not hurt me, I'll give in because they are showing me "love." The pull was strong, emotionally. But it was not within the purpose set before me.

Admittedly, it took a while before I released the training program with company 'C.' The leader that approached me was a trusted authority in the Air Force and in his current field. This person was diligent in his pursuit. I mean, his game was strong! And I would have enjoyed the continuous access to his wisdom, but it was not for me. It was difficult, but I disenrolled from the program. When we talked, he fully supported my way forward and offered support for the future. I was pleasantly surprised, and the encounter solidified the depth of our relationship.

My focus became increasingly narrowed. I set appointments with myself to update my files and online presence. At some point, I requested mentorship time with a few more city and town managers, a few of them offered to review my resume. One local town manager took special interest regarding my transition preparation. He gave me access to a state association's information and meetings. Even though our calendars did not sync as often as desired, it did not have a negative impact on our relationship.

June 2019: I received a call from an old friend, he told me of an opportunity with the company he was in. He was informing me of an expansion intent projected for the Summer of 2020. A whole year out! This time, it was not a true distraction. Training, development, and coaching is within my passion and giftedness, and this call was in line with that. The thing is, he wanted a resume to present to the company president in the same month. So, I clicked over and adjusted my files towards development. Although I knew this was not a near-term deal, it was a comparable career path for me.

What I did not realize, this would be the catalyst for me to have finalized documents to share with organizations. Remember my goal for August 2019? My first submission was in June. While on a business trip, describing my future career with my oldest daughter and my wife's friend, I saw a job posting in Texas that really was appealing. My first municipal application was submitted in July 2019. I didn't get the job, but I wasn't ready to transition. Beyond that, I expected to learn instead of win on that submission. I got a small piece of feedback, and from there, it was like letting blood in the water in shark infested water. My appetite was heightened, my documents were established, and my confidence escalated!

From there, I was submitting to jobs every month, improving my documents with each iteration. Did I mention my anticipated transition to be August 2020? It was important for me to discover the cycle length from advertisements through the new hire sitting in the seat. My research informed me of a four to six month timeline. This significantly shifted my approach and drive in the transition strategy. Many people leaving the military submit their retirement application one year in advance, due to the style of responsibility I was seeking, it was wise for me to not do a 12-month projection.

For every person it will be an "it depends" type of approach but let me tell you why I exercised the four-month minimum transition mindset.

When I spoke to a retired Air Force Colonel that served as the City Manager for Macon, Georgia, he asked me how much salary I would lose for the sake of three months, seeking the full 30-year retirement? Literally, how many hundreds of thousands of dollars incremented over the length of the next career am I willing to trade-in to get the words "long and" on a citation, and $17 per month more in my pension? This confirmed my tactic. For the relatively small number of opportunities, in a niche functional area, there are no predictable seasons for desirable opportunities. That said, I set timelines for where I would submit applications based on how long it may take to be selected, relative to the end of my contractual obligation. In other words, if I had to stay in the state I was in, with a high cost of living and housing market, when would I stop trying to stay "here"? My family could move to the area of preference, and I continued my search locally if I did not have any other options.

July to December 2019: I was very purposeful. I knew the content of the job boards I used. I could see the slightest changes each day to the sites. I worked hard to make my documents understandable by someone who never spoke to a military professional. My review of various city council meetings and city manager interviews or discussions was relentless. There was no quenching of my thirst for knowledge. In the local area, the city and town managers became more familiar with me and actually alerted me to projected vacancies. They would also inform me of the flavor of the local politics. Some places were considered tough, with fully engaged citizens, others were docile, while a few would be classified as contemptuous with high turnovers.

The method of evaluation took me to a deeper dive on culture and how I may "fit." If I applied for a location, beforehand, I wanted to learn how it may impact me emotionally or wear on my resiliency. This is more important than you think in the long run.

November 2019: I applied for several positions, had an interview in December 2019 and in January 2020, I was a finalist for the position that I now serve in. Contract negotiations began and work began in April. Please do not miss the timeline.

Let's walk it back to the vacancy and land on the report for work date. The incumbent gave notice and departed around July or August, the Town formed a search committee and hired a search firm. After building the community profile and establishing the goals for the new hire, the advertisement was posted in November. The candidate list was reduced to those that would receive invitation for the first round of interviews and those appointments occurred in December. The final round was completed in January, with a decision made the night of the interview. Contract negotiations went on for a few weeks and once we were agreeable, I rendered notice to depart my employment at that time.

My first day of work was in April 2020. From the time the previous town manager left until I showed up for work was nine months. It took nine months to birth this baby. I was passively preparing during the first few months, due to being informed that the vacancy was projected, and people encouraged me to watch for the opportunity. In reality, the advertisement through the final interview was a three-month process. Negotiations for the contract took almost two more months, then spending the requisite time required to depart the previous employment.

During the entire time that I was seeking opportunities, my goal was to discover what a realistic timeline could be. The reason this was important was largely due to the requirements associated with the career I was already in. Most jobs can accept a two-week resignation, that does not work for the Air Force. It was possible to project my transition four to twelve months in advance.

A great percentage of people do a 12-month projection, but I felt that would have been a flaw in the strategy, seeing that these types of vacancies are not as common as other professions. Based on the overall goal of changing employment no later than August 2020, keeping my options fluid became a blessing in the end. Had I been selected in January and not available until August, that may have become detrimental for the hiring authorities.

During all of this, I continued expanding my knowledge through formal education courses as well as training programs through the association. For the degree, increasing the number of classes per term became really important. Even though the offer for employment came, there was no way that the path to gain another degree would be hindered. The additional degree was completed in July 2020.

And things did not stop there! Do you remember the points from August 2018? There is still an unfulfilled item. In September 2020, the next goal was initiated. Having a municipal management certificate program completed was something I wanted done while in the first contract period. In May 2021, the goal was also accomplished.

At the time of this writing there remains the goal to get my master's in public administration. Rest assured that it is being addressed. Doing a gap analysis is a great exercise, but you have to do something with what you discover. Again, hope is not a plan, and a plan is not action. We have to put our feet under the words and plans, otherwise, it is just a dream. Wake up! Hope deferred makes the heart sick, according to a set of proverbs. In most cases, there is no active opposition to people's goals. Self-doubt, delays, procrastination, major life events, distractions and other discouraging factors get accepted and next thing you know, seven years have slipped by. You will discover, when you ponder the paths of your feet, knowing that every step matters, your progress will steadily manifest itself if you keep walking in the right direction.

6.

NAYSAYERS SAY...

SO

"SWEET ARE THE USES OF ADVERSITY..."

-William Shakespeare

One thing that you must prepare your mind for is that everyone will not be supportive of your transition, and some will go beyond failing to show support to actually being negative. You won't know their motive, and I encourage you not to try and figure out their motives. You will expend energy and time in an endeavor that will likely be fruitless, and you will be unable to recover the time and energy. But I must acknowledge that regardless of if it is an intentional or unintentional act, it hurts.

You must predetermine that you are going to be resilient. Naysayers say a lot of things, but so what? When naysayers pop up, you have to already be grounded in the fact you are confident of the direction of your transition. Knowing that you are following your calling or purpose gives you a steadfastness necessary to stay the course. If you are not rooted and grounded in what you believe prior to encountering a naysayer, the odds are high they may derail you, even if it is temporary. But when you know that you know, you should be able to stay the course. When you know that you know, in spite of the pain, you channel the negative input and use it as fodder to fuel your fire.

Naysayers may say, "You'll never get into that school," or, "You'll never get a scholarship," or, "They will never hire someone like you for that position," or, "You are not qualified." Again, I say, naysayers will say what they want, but so what?

KNOW UP FRONT SOME
WON'T BE SUPPORTIVE

To be completely honest, this is the part that really hurt! As I gained greater clarity on what I saw for my future, I was surprised at how some of my peers were not supportive. I expected there to be naysayers, but not from so many peers. I would share my vision and I would get comments like, "What makes you think you can do that?" or, "Chiefs don't do stuff like that," or, "Are you sure you could do that? What experiences from your past lend themselves to that?" Then there were officers I had worked with and I felt there was a mutual respect as leaders that had similar comments.

What many don't understand is that those of us in transition are fighting our own internal mental battles of doubt and fear and the additional negative input can put us on shaky ground. Now, I am not saying that you do not need people in your life to challenge your thought process to ensure you remain on track with your vision and to vet ideas. We all need a sound voice or two in our lives. But there is a huge difference in being a voice of reason and being a voice that questions. One encourages us while sharpening us. The other only plants seeds of doubt. Make sure you can distinguish between the two.

You must also be prepared for a naysayer to be a part of your inner circle, a spouse, a close friend or relative. I was fortunate that once my wife understood the vision, she was supportive. She could see in me what I saw in myself. When I said Chief Operating Officer, she didn't scoff. That was critical for me! She didn't know it at the time, but this was some much-needed rebar to help fortify the structure I was attempting to build. But what do you do if your situation is not like mine? What if it is your spouse who is the chief naysayer? What if your best friend becomes your antagonist? As tough as it is, you have to guard your heart and your vision.

You may not be able to share with them what you see, especially in the early stages. You will need to intentionally seek out someone else in whom you can confide and get encouragement. And at the same time, don't hold it against them, especially if it is your spouse. They may just need a little more time to see what you see.

GUARD YOUR HEART

Meriam-Webster.com defines "guard" as this: one assigned to protect or oversee another a defensive state or attitude the act or duty of protecting or defending defensively watchful: ALERT.[10]

For the context of this book, we will focus on the latter definition. You have to take precautions to protect your heart from being injured by a naysayer. But how do you do that? First thing is intentionality. Once you know that someone is not supportive, regardless of how you perceive the relationship, you have been intentional not to share your dreams with them. At the present time they don't get it and because they don't get it, they can be a dream stealer. They don't understand that comments like, "That will never work," reverberate around your head for hours, days, and weeks after the conversation. These negative comments are truly like Kryptonite. They can be truly paralyzing, so you must avoid sharing your enthusiasm and excitement with them.

Now with that said, you also must grow to

the point where you do not take the negative comments personally. You have to be like a duck and let the water roll off your back. The bottom line is, they cannot see what you see, because it was not meant for them to see what you see. Otherwise, they would see it. I know, that sounds simple, but pause and let it sink in. It's okay that they don't see it. What matters the most is that *you* see it! Don't let bitterness creep into your heart. Bitterness is like cancer and no amount of cancer in our heart is good.

Next, you need to have a trusted circle. This is the place where you can share all of your dreams and hopes in an unfettered way. These are the people who encourage you when you are doubting yourself (fire lighters). These are the ones that will give you sound advice and course corrections as needed. These are the people who blow air under your wings and desire to see you succeed as much as you desire to succeed. These are the people who see your win and their win.

Third, you have to be absolutely resolute in what you believe. You have to know that you know that you are on the right track in your pursuits. I am not advocating blindly chasing a dream, but after you have vetted your dreams and plans, you have to pursue them doggedly and that does not occur if you are not convinced that you are on the right path. And when you know that you know, I encourage you to speak your goals out loud to yourself. You must channel all of your "inner talk" or "self-talk" to be congruent with your goals and objectives. Often in our lives this cognitive dissonance is the culprit that undermines dreams and goals.

Fourth, I encourage you to use the shopping cart method. This means when you walk down the aisle in the grocery store, you do not put everything on the shelf in your cart. The only things you put in your cart are the things that you need, and you leave everything else on the shelf. Use this method with the naysayers as they may have something of use embedded in their negative comment. Use this method with those in your circle who are positive because something that worked for them may not work for you in the exact same way.

DON'T TAKE IT PERSONALLY

This is much easier said than done. How can I sit here and tell you not to take it personally when some of the negativity will come from people who are either family members, friends, or peers? Words have the ability to cut deep. And if it were only one cut, we would heal and keep it moving, but because we rehearse words over and over in our minds, they continue to cut and at times it seems as if they cut deeper each time. We struggle to maintain our own positive self-talk. We fight off negative thoughts in our own mind and then someone close reinforces a thought we had. What are you talking about Mac? Don't take it personally? Are you for real? That doesn't make any sense. That is illogical.

Yea I know. I get it. I understand your pushback. I've been there. Again, thank GOD for my wife! I took blows from a lot of people I did not expect to take blows. The bottom line is, you are doing it for you and not for them. If you take it personal, you will allow the seed of bitterness to be planted into your heart and mind. Bitterness is a weed and all weeds do is take nutrients away from the plants we desire to see grow. Choose not to take it personal, release it and grow the seeds of what you see after your transition. Refuse to give any nutrients to negativity. Taking it personally is negativity. You are bigger than that. You are better than that. They don't quite understand what you understand. Again, they don't see what you see, and they won't see it until after it manifests for you. Leaders see first and leaders see farther. It's okay to think about the day when they will see it and be supportive, because in many cases they are not deliberately against you.

Furthermore, many times the words of doubt are not intended to be words of doubt, nor are they intended to hurt you. In some cases, these words are formed out of a sincere place of friendship or deeper relationship. They believe they are helping to protect you from getting hurt. They don't want to see you fail and experience the ensuing pain they perceive is inevitably on the backside of failure. And in reality, in many cases, these individuals are projecting their own fears of failure and the inevitable pain onto you. They are trapped in their mind from ever doing something beyond what they are doing and so someone within their circle attempting to do this is scary to them. Because if you succeed, you potentially destroy most of their reasons for not being able to triumphantly transition to something else.

If you succeed, their foundation has a severe crack that threatens the totality of their structure. This is very scary and causes many people to default to a "fear reaction," which is seen by their words. Jay-Z said in an interview that his uncle told him that he would never sell a million records when he first started his rap career instead of being a street hustler. (Note: This is a major transition, and boy was it a triumphant transition.) Jay-Z went on to say, "I sold a million records like a million times."[9] He also said that he did not believe his uncle had any malice in his heart towards him. His uncle was just projecting his fears. I will refer back to a previous statement, it is *your* vision. The person projecting the fear and doubt, cannot see what you see. It is *your* vision. Hold fast to the vision or dream!

SHOPPING CART METHOD

When you go into a grocery store, you don't usually walk down the aisle and take one of everything on the shelf and put it in your cart. That would lead to a very expensive grocery bill. Instead, we typically make a list and then we purchase the things that we need and the temptations at the checkout counter. When you get input from naysayers there may be something for you to glean to help you in your transition. Use this method. Take what you need or can use and leave the rest. And when I say leave the rest, I mean do not allow it to take up residence in your mind and heart. Leave it on the shelf.

7.

FIRE LIGHTERS, FIREFIGHTERS AND FIRE PITS

Who surrounds you? Who is feeding your soul and ambitions? What are the people in your circle saying? How are their words impacting you?

Bishop Thomas Dexter (T.D.) Jakes has a message where he teaches about firefighters and fire lighters. In his assessment, fire lighters will jeopardize your dreams and vision. Your momentum can be stifled or stopped by a firefighter.

Conversely, Bishop Jakes indicates that a fire lighter will add fuel to your fire, bring kindling or logs. Said differently, these are the people that will encourage others, challenge them to do better and press past existing limitations.

We will take it a bit further and add the concept of the fire pit. Fire pit people don't mind the heat and light as long as you do not go too far or grow too big, others can benefit from you, and you don't proceed beyond the limits placed on you from the user's viewpoint.

FIRE FIGHTERS

As I came near the end of my military obligation, as we all do in some way or another, I found myself evaluating what could be next – and when. When I was selected to move to Hanscom Air Force Base, Massachusetts, I had exactly three years remaining in my uniformed service. This meant that I would have to do some other job or contribution to society afterwards. What I did as a result of this truth was I began to prepare. Not in an overt way. I did not want to be what they call R.O.A.D. – retired on active duty. Finding out what I wanted to be when I grew up never really occurred to me up to this point. I had ideas, but nothing captured my full attention...yet.

So, I worked on my leadership approach and mindset, making small adjustments to how I processed information, developed others and ways to draw more out of the teams I served. This actually became a great exercise. My personal motto is "Leaders Lead." And that is what I wanted from others, for them to become better leaders.

Instead of being super prescriptive, my goal was to invite greatness out of others in a different and purposeful way.

In the set of responsibilities I had, preparing airmen to navigate through the tough decision-making process of leaving the uniform or reenlisting (continuing their contract) was nearly a monthly engagement. Unlike many senior leaders, my approach was always centered on reality and preparation.

It was time for me to apply the things I repeatedly said to others, do a realistic assessment, ask hard questions, make a decision and move forward. Once the direction for my 'next' was set, it was important to seek and gain support along the way. It was absolutely critical to me to have people I could bounce ideas off of, get encouragement when needed and have true accountability with. When I started talking about my ideas of the future, what I encountered almost threw me off.

Naturally, some people were very supportive, but a few of the ones I valued made me scratch my head. One person, a newer mentor in my career, indicated that my ambitions were lofty. So lofty that it was likely out of reach. One day, he asked me to come see him. During the conversation he told me it might be wise to stop talking about my post-uniform goals to others. What if I failed to attain them? What would be the impact on the junior airmen? I didn't know what to say at first. What was I to tell people when they asked me direct questions about plans after the military? How could I not live by the guidance I have given to others?

Another person that I spoke with on a very frequent basis said that we are not built for those types of jobs, or something to that effect. He went so far as to say that I should simply do like most others and seek a federal government position somewhere. I recognized these two encounters as fire fighters. They were quick to boost me up and encourage me in military activities, but as I drew closer to retirement, the more our interactions seemed different. It was time to reduce the impact of their words. They had become firefighters. The words they chose were likely not intended to be detrimental. Heck, they were even said in an upbeat way. Yet the impact was not aligned with their intent of being positive.

It seemed as if my energy was drained whenever the topic of transition came up. What really trips me out is, they would be the ones that brought it up. At some point, I figured, this is not what I need to continuously hear. So, I avoided the topic with them. There was no need to sever a relationship. It wasn't that serious! But I refused to have the flames of my future doused by people I trusted. I'm not sure why their words were formulated the way they were, and that did not matter to me. I assessed it as them trying to prevent a deep disappointment if I missed the mark. Potentially a good motivation, but firefighter, nonetheless.

FIRE LIGHTERS

On the other hand, through my friends and colleagues, a large number of people caught the vision of what could be accomplished in my future. Even strangers became cheerleaders and champions in my corner. In an effort to learn more about the industry of interest, I reached out to a person on LinkedIn. What started as a random connection request, based on his military background, turned into a lasting, mutually beneficial relationship both personally and professionally. There was one person that really blessed me throughout the process. He had recently gone through a military retirement and understood the importance of staying focused and getting the right support along the way. These people were fire lighters!

They kept stoking the flames by telling me to keep on task. They held me accountable to my words and intent. When times were tough and I drifted towards distractions, they identified the perceived hazards. When the inevitable low points hit, these were the brothers and sisters I could lean on to lift me up and to redirect negative energy and thoughts. We all need these types of people to prevent perpetually destructive distractions.

FIRE PITS

I feel inclined to share regarding another set of people that you may overlook. These seem to be influencers in a dual role. This includes the duality of encouragement and limitation. Unfortunately, this often feels like or is a somewhat slighted engagement. I have seen some leaders pump up others, until they perceive there could be advancement beyond where they are. They are willing to support you as long as you benefit them in some way or another. They wish to contain your success in a measurable fashion. Sometimes it is covert. Other times it may be a default setting within them, and they really have no malicious intent. These are fire pit people.

But wait. There is someone else in the fire pit category at times. It's you! If you are a pleaser, insecure, self-destructive, or a glory hog, you may build or reinforce fire pit principles. In fact, you may apply these limitations to yourself, often in a subliminal way. You must be cautious of the trap to apply limits within your own heart and mind. Avoid ceiling heights that you create. Furthermore, as you seek to please or impress others, watch out for the invitations and inquiries into restrictive and boxed opportunities. Far too many times, you willingly enter a self-containing environment called the fire pit. From this point on, don't block your own blessings.

Evaluate the impact of those that surround you. Discover who is feeding your soul and ambitions, as opposed to those draining your productive energy. Pay close attention to what the people in your circle are saying. If it is not the right thing, have a conversation to identify the situation or need, that may be the best path to resolving any issues that creep up. Be careful of how the words of others are impacting you. If necessary, create a bit more space between the interactions.

There is a statement that I have come to know to be true for every single person walking this earth no matter where you are on the earth. The statement is this: Our input determines our thoughts; our thoughts determine our action; our actions determine our habits; our habits determine our character; and our character determines our destiny.

I don't care who you are, the statement applies. So how does this apply to firefighters, fire lighters, and fire pits? Stay with me, I'm going somewhere. We receive our input through one of two gates: eye-gate (what we look at consistently) and our ear-gate (what we listen to consistently). Who we surround ourselves with (friend-gate) will have a great influence on what goes into our ear- and eye-gates.

It has been said, "Show me your five closest friends and I will show you your future." Be cognizant of who you have surrounding you. Are they a firefighter? How about a fire pit? Or perhaps they are a fire lighter? Correctly identify them and make the tough decision(s). As HH mentioned above, you don't have to sever the relationship—although you may have to depending on how negative they are—just put some space between you and them. Don't worry about what they may think in this season. In times of transition, your energy and focus needs to be on transitioning triumphantly. Once this season is over, if they are a true friend, they will be there, And if they are not, oh well.

Lastly, there is a saying that indicates that a person can be "snared by the words of their mouth." Don't let that be you. Do not be the firefighter in your own transition. What do I mean by this? I am talking about your self-talk. Self-talk is the thing you say in your head that no one else can hear but you. We talk to ourselves more than anyone in the world. Don't let your own voice be the voice to quench the fire of your passion to pursue what you see. What you say to you matters the most.

SIDEBAR #2:
FEEDBACK MAY STING AT FIRST, BUT PUSH PAST THE PAIN

"Faithful are the wounds of a friend, But the kisses of an enemy are deceitful."

Proverbs 27:6 (NKJV)

This became a reality for me during my preparation phase regarding my resume. I have a friend (during the process it almost became 'had' a friend) in the industry that I was interested in that I asked to review my documents. We have similar enough first careers towards our final position before our contracts ended. I knew he would understand my writing and be able to identify opportunities for conversion language or rephrasing of terms. I was right, but his method put me in shock. Let me tell you what he did, this is sharing, not complaining. At least it's not complaining anymore.

Picture this: I worked for a few months to remove or change much of the jargon and organizational terms from my first version of a resume. This guy gave me some great feedback, up to the point he told me, "What is this? That means nothing to me," or words to that effect. He was talking about some recognition that was a big deal in my prior profession. When I pushed back, he held his position. My frustration caused me to virtually get in his face and get him to acknowledge the award. What he said next floored me with truth. His "position" had no clue what that accomplishment was or how to assess value to it; therefore, it gets no worth assigned. I'm sure he knew that his tactic and delivery would disturb me, but he was very effective with it. So, I cauterized the wound, made the adjustments and kept it moving. Had I allowed myself to get twisted and walk away from him or rejected the wisdom being shared, I may not have received the message and invaluable lessons we discussed during that time. And who knows, I may not be contributing to this work that you are reading.

I went to him because of our relationship and the trust I had for him. I knew that he traveled the path I wanted to go on. He was a hiring authority, and he understood both sides of the assessment. Those nine minutes of frustration turned into a revenue stream that...wait, let me back off of that before he asks for a cut.

Seriously, don't be so prideful with the feedback you receive, especially from someone you respect and trust. The method of delivery is important, but if you don't appreciate the style, hang in there a while, it may be purposeful and beneficial to you in the long run. As I see it, the wounds of a friend are faithful. For that, I'm grateful.

Before we go further. Let's look at another analogy. For those familiar with lifting weights, there is the need to have a spotter in certain instances. This person is to help in times of trouble and when the bar is too heavy or the situation gets dangerous. This rarely ends up with the rescue being needed, but the spotter is an automatic safety measure put in place. Most of the time, the use of the spotter is for encouragement.

I remember too many times being under the bar, as well as being the spotter. As the one lifting the weight, there were moments when I would desperately say, "Okay. Get it," as a request for help due to my fatigue or pain. Do you think the spotter instantly took the bar from me? Nope! Most cases, I heard, "You got it. Come on. I got you," as a response. There was no time to argue, I had more than 100+ pounds hovering over my neck and chest, so I pushed. Sometimes I shifted my feet, other times I would strain and break my form by arching my back, to which I would get a sharp correction. Don't you see me struggling, just take the weight! Again, I would hear, "You got it. Push. Push."

During this ordeal of me getting the bar up and being told to push, I notice something interesting, and possibly frightening if I give it too much attention. The spotter only had four fingers on the bar. You can't rescue me with four fingers. But the spotter is in the right position, has oversight of the total situation, has the leverage required, perceives the effort and energy I have to give and is ever ready to intervene. If I got to total failure, the bar may actually touch me before being removed, but it won't crush me. It's a scary thought, but it won't crush me. And again, I hear, "Push!" So, I push. It is hard and uncomfortable.

I feel like I cannot do it. I fear my arms giving out or being injured. But I push. I may even hear a second voice of encouragement from a nearby lifter. And I push. And the bar raises. And the four fingers look like just what I needed at the moment, and I push. At great relief, the bar is up high enough, and I feel the tug to get the weight over the resting place for safety. Whew! We did it!

But wait, the spotter did not do what I really think they did. Were those four fingers really helping me as much as it seemed? Or was I simply being yelled at by someone straddling my head? Did I just get tricked? After lifting for a while, we know the spotter did not do that much work physically, it was mainly presence, mental reassurance, and readiness to respond. In the end, who gets up from the bench and confronts the spotter saying, "You tricked me, put my life at risk, and yelled at me unnecessarily"? Who does that?

In reality, there is a mini celebration and appreciation. A small break is taken, and then we get after it or switch positions. Now that I am the spotter, do I render the help I wanted while under the bar or the service of being in position if the true need arises? So, there I was. "Push. You got it!"

We cannot allow ourselves to abandon the gains we seek when our spotter challenges us to give a little more effort. When others see more strength than we feel, we should trust it in the same way as if our back was on the bench. Trust the four fingers, respond to the command to push, and ignore the fact that they are straddling your head!

Lifting weight is about getting stronger and increasing fitness, but it happens by being in a controlled setting, with safeguards in place. This process includes being under pressure and resistance, literally creating micro-tears, resting properly and healing. With the right nourishment and hydration, the micro-tears heal and thicken the muscle fibers. And the process is repeated. Do not abandon the process. Recognize the micro-tears are for your benefit if the nutrients and hydration are in order. Faithful are the wounds of a friend.

SIDEBAR #3:
SPEAK THE TRUTH IN LOVE

So, I was the "friend" referred to in the paragraphs above. And I must say that before I gave the feedback I thought long and hard about what I would say because I valued and still value our friendship. He has provided wise counsel to me on several occasions, and he is my confidant. I did not want to offend or insert any schism into the relationship. I valued the relationship, but I also wanted to add value to my friend. I wanted to provide feedback that I knew in my heart that could help him to be successful since our worlds were so similar. It was tough but I decided to go ahead and proceed with the feedback I thought would be beneficial. His resume was sound if he was applying for a job on a military installation or a Department of Defense contractor, as they are very familiar with the terms and with the significance of his awards and accomplishments as many are led by veterans or have veterans in senior leadership roles that can translate.

He was applying for a job where the hiring authority had limited knowledge of the military in a very general sense but were not keenly familiar with the terms and references in his resume. I knew full well the significance of the awards and accomplishments that he listed in his resume, but I knew from two years of experience in my new role that the people he would be working for did not grasp the significance. This could lead to them overlooking a very qualified candidate that could help to take them to the next level. I knew his past experience and phenomenal leadership skills would add value to the organization, so my feedback to him came out of a very sincere desire to see him succeed.

In addition to having a measure of understanding in the area into which he was attempting to gain access, I also was a hiring authority and had reviewed a number of resumes, to include some from transitioning military personnel. The majority of the ones I reviewed succumbed to the same mistake; they failed to adequately translate their past experiences and make them relevant to the industry they sought. When I finished putting my input on the document, this is what I put in the email, "If you disregard my input, no offense taken. If you want to chat, for me to explain my thoughts let me know." I had determined if he did not take my input that it was okay, and he was still my friend. An example of the feedback I gave him is as follows.

One section of the resume:

Academic Affairs Superintendent
(Education and Talent Development Manager)
Instructor / Curriculum Writer, Squadron Officer
College (Officer Professional Military Education)

My feedback:

"I know this is what you want to emphasize, but I don't know that the hiring manager will be interested in the fact you ran a school."

Now what he did as an enlisted person was a very big deal as he was involved in a senior role in the development of officers in the United States Air Force. But as presented it was not relevant to the position he was seeking. I know he busted his tail excelling at this job and I knew he had great pride in all that he had accomplished, so I knew it would sting. This is where I had to decide if I was going to provide honest feedback or not. Another example is one line on the resume that read:

"Improved international exchanges, conference with British, Japanese, Spanish and Israeli officials on professional development and aircraft maintenance practices within officer and enlisted populations."

The bottom line was I wanted to be an ally in his quest for entry into this new realm. Over the course of his hiring process, I was right there with him in his highs and lows. There were times during his process that I would get so excited or angry that one might have thought I was the one applying for the position. I was truly in it with him and sought the entire time to be an additional support.

Context: To be selected to work with a foreign military is a high honor. In the armed forces we do not put our struggling performers or poor performers in these roles. People selected for these roles are what we call "high speed and low drag." They are very high performers! I asked my friend:

Below is an example of the feedback I provided:

How did you do this?
What was your role?
Why was this important?
What happens if you don't do this?
Tell me why I should care.

Again, I was not being flippant, but I felt what he intended to communicate was not being communicated. Of note, I did not tell him what he should write. He is a very intelligent individual and he did not need me to hold his hand. All he needed was a nudge in the right direction. A point to those who are in positions of providing feedback, if the person requires more than a nudge, if they require hand holding, be careful. This gives us a feeling of being needed and we can step in and help too much and thus cause them to short-circuit the development process.

8.

IMPORTANCE OF NETWORKING

WHAT IS NETWORKING?

When you read the word "networking," what did you think? For real?

- Professional manipulation
- Brown nosing
- Kissing up to people
- Compromising for self-gain
- Being fake in order to seek favors

None of those things sound right to those with high moral and ethical standards. Many people feel relationships and interactions should be natural. I largely agree. But only to a point. Before we go too far, let's look at the term itself.

A definition of "networking," according to the Merriam-Webster Dictionary, is "the exchange of information or services among individuals, groups, or institutions; specifically: the cultivation of productive relationships."[10] Other sources may include inferences to social or professional settings or goals.

Exchange or share wisdom, knowledge, or

understanding. Nothing wrong so far. This includes services as an exchange potential. We all have bartered before, at some level. To cultivate productive relationships. Cultivation is commonly known as an agricultural word. This is not the situation where spreading manure equals super growth. Productive is an indicator that the goal is not to waste time on non-impacting matters.

Keep in mind, non-impacting is one of those 'eye of the beholder' items. In some cultures, efficiency of effort is championed, while in other places significant weight is placed on how the leader 'feels' about the other person and their assessment of their character. May you be wise in your dealings.

GET PAST YOUR FEELINGS

Still not feeling the whole networking thing, that's fine, took me a minute too. I take you back to previous responsibilities and positions. I remember interactions with foreign military leaders, city and state officials, tribal dignitaries, clergy and various corporate authorities and representatives. Although we are not on the list to celebrate children's birthdays, we spent time getting to know each other. We also almost always talked about projects or goals that either side could contribute towards success.

Somehow, using the same logic is offensive to some. Don't let your feelings fool you. You have got to play by the rules of the game that you're in. I will share two experiences you may encounter.

In 2018, I reached out to a stranger on LinkedIn. Greg accepted the connection request and subsequently agreed to a phone conversation. I had nothing to offer him of value, but I wanted to hear about his experiences, transition and discover any recommendations he may have. After the first conversation, we figured that we could talk again in the future. I was grateful, plus he told me about a webinar that would be happening in November. I attended the webinar and discovered that Greg was one of the presenters.

Greg and I formed a friendly relationship, it actually felt natural. My initial attention was drawn to him purely as a result of a search in the system. And truthfully, I had nothing to offer him other than prayer. Greg was very open with me, he listened and provided great discussion, I was very appreciative. During some of the conversations, we learned more of commonalities and challenges. At a certain point, we would reach out to each other (primarily me purposefully engaging) as a check in over the next year. During one of our conversations, after I was hired and working, I was able to offer this experienced City Manager advice related to his contract renewal. From the onset, I imagined that I had nothing to bring to the table that would bless Greg in a tangible way. Because we developed a level of trust, he opened up in a way that allowed me to contribute to his situation.

Greg and I are still in communication and what started as a blind outreach, seemingly randomly selected, based on his military experience, turned into a mutually beneficial and long-lasting interaction. People are often hesitant to connect with those they don't know, or they are too aggressive in the initial interaction, expecting the other party to give you the keys to their house on the first meeting. Networking can be a delicate balancing act at times. When done properly, it is a great way to expand your circle of friendship, influence, and knowledge.

TAKE PEOPLE AT THEIR WORD

I'll share another set of thoughts I once had.
I thought networking could potentially be a
disingenuous way to use people for what you
can get from them. This is the wrong way to view
the concept and that the way it flows is largely
based on the characteristics and perspective of
the people in the conversation. The way we view a
thing determines how we see a thing, and in turn,
it influences our actions. Here is an example of
how my perspective had to change on the topic.
Keep in mind that I had "informational interviews"
prior to being appointed in the position I now have.

People told me to reach out to them if
I had any questions, I took this as a simple
encouragement that had no substance. Besides,
everyone is busy, right? The offer is just the proper
thing to do. I mean, if someone directly connected
me with another person, I would reach out once to
see if there was any interest by them. Other than
that, hard or cold networking was like trying to get
a sneak peek into a process through people that
you don't know. I have no interest in that.

Eventually I got a revelation. Just follow through. The way I did things in the past was, if a person reached out to me, they had to be the one to seek and secure the communication. I did not chase people down to give them information. But if they did their part, I had no problem sharing information with them. I just stopped short of trying to make them feel as if I was going to own or take over their portions of responsibility going forward. I needed to reflect and taste my own words. So, I committed to following through with an offer for conversation.

Pete told me twice to shoot him a text or call. So, I did. Pete was in another state on vacation, and he asked me to call him back in a few minutes. When I did, he was driving. The conversation was so good, and he wanted to express some things clearly, he actually pulled over, and we finished about an hour more of discussion. While he was on vacation! At the end of the call he asks, "Have you talked to Nate?" I hadn't. Again, I thought that offer was out of courtesy. My next action—text Nate. Guess what, Nate was serious about wanting to talk.

Nate was a bit more old-school and structured towards in-person interaction. When he offered a lunch appointment, I said, "Yes," even before checking my calendar or the location. Turns out, I had to change a few other things around because Nate's preferred location to meet was almost two hours away. He knew the distance for me to drive, and it may have been a test of "how bad do you want it." But I was up for it. That morning, there was a snowstorm. I thought about postponing, but I felt the pressure of time as I was soon to be interviewed and wanted to get more advice before the interview. So, I pressed my way through the storm, it took a little over two hours because of the heavy snow coming down. I arrived at the location before Nate and became familiar with the menu and layout, so I did not seem unsure of my selections and options when he arrived.

Meeting Nate that day was definitely a huge blessing! He had a lot of experience in the field I wanted to explore, he seemed genuine in the interaction about believing I could go forward into the career type, and he was easy to talk to. He did pose some scenarios to me to see how I assessed them in the past and going into the future. I was warned about how easy it is to offend people by using the wrong terminology. I was inspired to dig deeper in my preparation for the interview. My confidence increased due to the confirmation I received in the conversations. And to imagine, I was not going to talk with Pete or Nate, thinking they were just being cordial with the offer to talk. Now that I am reflecting on it, I was told by a few people, repeatedly, "Give me a call," "Shoot me a text," "Here's my number, don't be shy," "We should talk soon," "If you have any questions, don't hesitate." I mean it when I say it, why did I doubt others?

I was blocking myself regarding opportunities to talk with other professionals and thought leaders. It won't happen that way again. And you should stop getting in the way of your own goals and connection potentials. Funny how we reject the very things we offer to others by saying, "Yeah, but…" to that I tell you to get your "but…" out of the way.

NETWORKING TOOLS

Using the tools and apps as platforms:

• **Beyond the resume (extension of):** What your resume does not say, can be identified on LinkedIn. I used the articles portion to express the way I think in a concise and clear way. It can also demonstrate your writing skills, creativity, and leadership perspective. You can provide potential business partners, employers, and clients with a view of your insight, approach to various challenges, express your logic and display your character. If you have an alphabet soup behind your name, establish a section to outline and describe those items. This can be done for any abbreviations.

• **Connections:** For those in a relatively tight circle or industry, this platform can rapidly expand your reach. I encourage people to build a solid profile well before they intend to use it as a tool for seeking employment. This way you do not feel rushed or pressure. Take your time, build a network of people you know and don't.

Yes, include friends, but expand beyond just them. Even if you are only connecting for the job similarity, it could one day benefit both people involved through idea sharing.

• **Training:** Personal and professional growth is a never-ending quest. Some hiring authorities like to see or perceive the commitment to enhancing one's knowledge. This could be an area where this tool becomes a superior method of enrichment. Training is offered and can be displayed in this forum.

• **Job leads:** This function can be visible to others, or not. Some people are cautious about others knowing they are seeking opportunities; I can respect that. If you set the system properly, only you will be notified of potential jobs that you could have interest in and nobody else will be the wiser.

• **Beacon for headhunters to find and consider you:** Hiring agents and headhunters will review your profile, especially if you have an adequate profile and some relative content that they are looking for. Yes, I recognize that you may have had a sensitive job if you did government work, but that can be worked out. You have done a lot of leading, deciding, problem solving in and outside of the sensitive parts. The quest then becomes about how you allow others to grow to know you without revealing sensitive matters. It is possible.

Professional networking applications can be utilized with those in the local area or 3,092 miles away. It closes the distance gap rather quickly. Just take note of the time zones for appointments.

QUICK TIPS ON CONNECTING WITH PEOPLE YOU DO NOT KNOW

- Use the invitation with a message
- Don't ask for much, especially when you first reach out
- Discover what their story is and take notes
- Find a connection point or commonality
- Ask no more than three questions per session, send them in advance of a conversation
- Set a timer for limited interactions, if you are given 17 minutes, set your timer to remind you to close at the 14-minute mark
- Plant seeds towards a future appointment
- Put it on your calendar with notes and follow up
- Do not lie about connections between you and other people!

I have got to tell you about referring to other people and how we are connected. In May 2021, I had conversations with two strangers, Andy and Jack. Andy sent me a message and mentioned James as a reason he was reaching out to me. James is good people, but I don't remember having contact in quite a while. I agreed to set an appointment to talk with Andy. This young man went straight into fact gathering and rapid-fire questioning. At one point I stopped and asked him about James and there was silence. I figured I would cut him some slack and reminded him that he mentioned James in his first note to me. His eloquence fell short. So, I told him to be careful, somebody like me may scratch at the name you drop. I understand the hustle to get someone to talk to you—been there done that—but not being forthright may yield you attention you don't want or need.

Jack was referred to me by a mutual connection. They spoke and my name came up, then Stan sent me a note to indicate he wanted us to connect, if possible. I had a conversation with Jack for 36 minutes while at work, I typically won't take certain calls at work, but because Stan linked us up, I yielded. Based on the flow of the discussion, I offered Jack more time over the weekend. Jack accepted the offer and we spoke again at length the same weekend. And I am willing to speak with him again. He is putting in the work and not simply looking for an easy button.

CONNECTIONS, MENTORS/COACHES, SPONSOR, FRIENDS

• **Know the differences.** Greg was willing to review documents and provide feedback, but he would not serve as a reference for me. Why? His role was not to sponsor me, He was to be a mentor. Chris is my friend that could coach me but was not able to sponsor me in a different state. Nate, on the other hand, has the capability to sponsor me in the region I am in, based on his connections and how he is a leader within and across the industry.

• **Don't try to force anything.** The people that will talk to you may not give you all of the answers you desire in 17-34 minutes, or even an hour. You might really want to know something that they really won't talk about to a stranger. Try too hard and your next request to talk will be rejected.

• **Don't be quick to give up on people.** We are all busy. You did not rise to the top of the priority this week. Why? Because I don't know you, and I'm busy. Nothing against you. But if you want my attention, reach out again. But before you do, check your subject line for the email or first sentence on the message. When you do get an appointment, prepare for 15-30 minutes maximum. If it is with me, I should not have to remind you of the time allotted. You should respect the time carved out and initiate the hard stop.

CLEAN UP YOUR ONLINE PRESENCE

• **Remove distractions.** What would you not want your next hiring agent to see? Simply live your online life in that way and you may have nothing to worry about.

• **Use your name as it would appear on your resume.** Actually insert the middle initial if it will be on your resume. Why? How many Jeff Roberts are there on LinkedIn? Now check to see how many Jeff Z. Roberts are registered. Or Jeff Z. Roberts Jr. The list of potential association errors narrows rather quickly. You want the next employer to find you, not to get frustrated looking for your account.

• **Look at your photos on all social media.** This includes when people tag you. Should you really keep the image up of you drinking alcohol in your vehicle while you are seeking a public safety or transportation job?

• **Be careful what you post.** Everything is controversial. For real, everything. But what is over the top or a distraction if an employer saw it while you are a candidate? Is your style to be antagonistic with friends online? Do you allow vulgar language on your site? It is your site, but it is publicly accessible. Might a viewer estimate that you do not value other people based on protected categories and classes of others? If that is who you are, or your style of banter with friends, you may consider not having the profile name match your resume name.

• **Search your name online.** I found my name, I also found news clippings, biographies from bases I was assigned to, a dude that murdered someone, obituaries, a guy with way more money than me, my dad - all with the same first and last name. One time, there was a man with my first and last name in the next city that was overdue on the electricity bill. Different middle initial, but at first glance of the name, I was thought to be him. In fact, I have a going away gift with the wrong middle initial because there were two of us on the same email system with different middle initials. Funny enough, we are both 'Jr.' too!

For those that are skeptical of the online tools like LinkedIn, it is your choice to use it or not. If you are worried about your information being available to others and being mishandled, you are right. The chance exists. But similar risk is present if you are connected to the internet in any capacity, ever. Besides, this is a way for you to shape the narrative about you, in a professional, yet social environment.

If you are still anti-networking, again, your choice. Perhaps it is the way you are seeing it. I challenge you to change your angle on it. Set your parameters of what you will not do, and how to preserve your integrity and efforts. Regardless, of how you go forward, just move forward.

9.

DARE
TO
DREAM
BIG

**"DREAM NO SMALL DREAMS FOR THEY HAVE
NO POWER TO MOVE THE HEARTS OF MEN."**

-Johann Wolfgang von Goethe

IMPOSSIBLE OR IMPROBABLE

What is in the realm of the possible? Who defines what is possible? What did people think about flight before the Wright Brothers flew? What did people think about a motorized car before Henry Ford built the Model T? What did people think about Walt Disney when he presented the idea of an animated cartoon? What is the point? Dream big!

Why can't it be you? Why not you? What is it that is deep down inside your heart that when you have time and space you dream about? That thing that makes your heart race when you envision yourself doing it. What is it? What is that thing that you envision that you could do all day and never get tired. (Okay, maybe you could do it for a large part of your day and not get tired.) Dare to dream big.

I believe that inside each of us there are gifts of greatness and yes, I said gifts and not a gift. What if you dared to dream big and find a way to bring those gifts to the surface? How might the world be impacted? I will state again that I am convinced that everyone who is drawing breath has gifts to share. If there was no reason (purpose), you would have ceased to draw breath. I firmly believe for the world to maximize its potential we all need to share our gifts with the rest of the world. As we share our gifts with the world—your family, your neighborhood, your office, wherever you have influence—we begin to illuminate the world and make it better. So, dream big. Why not you?

If you have been a stay-at-home parent for the past six to ten years and you have raised some decent human beings that are prospering at their respective levels in life, why can't you run your own business or move into the executive suite? Anyone with kids knows leadership, planning, anticipation, and ability to adjust on a dime are inherent qualities of being a successful stay at home parent. Why not you?

If you're a teacher in a particular discipline and you have taught for years and you know your content areas extremely well, why can't you take the leap to move into corporate America or the non-profit arena in your field of expertise? Why not you?

If you are a student who came out of difficult circumstances and completed four years of high school with a stellar GPA, why can't you be successful at that prestigious school you have dreamed about. You had the discipline to focus and work hard despite the distractions from your circumstances. Why not you?

If you have been an executive assistant for a number of years and you have a heart to start a non-profit, why not you? Anyone with half a brain knows the executive assistant, when they are skilled at their craft, are a vital part of organizational success and they utilize numerous skills to facilitate that success. They do their thing quietly in the background, often using the "Jedi Mind Trick." What is the Jedi Mind Trick? When I have an idea and I talk to you, and you walk away thinking it is your idea. In this process they are not concerned that you think it is your idea. They are skilled in the art of leadership, which at its most basic definition is nothing other than influence. Why not you?

DARE TO BELIEVE

There is an ancient text that says something along the lines of GOD can do anything. If you believe in GOD, then why not take Him at His word? If we choose to believe, then "all" truly means "all." Look at some of the examples. David, because he believed, took down a seasoned war veteran that was a humongous giant with a sling and a stone. Gideon, because he believed, took 300 men and defeated his enemies, who were as numerous as the locusts. Moses, because he believed, parted the Red Sea. Joshua, because he believed, brought his people into the promised land. What is stopping you from believing? The book that I read also says that GOD is not a respecter of persons, which means He does *not* discriminate. GOD does not show personal favoritism. What He does for one, He can do for another. So why not you?

Finally, in spite of the real obstacles that may stand in your way, like not having the capital you need or access to the right influencers, you should not be discouraged. The ancient text that I read states that GOD will give you favor with people in addition to Himself. So, all we have to do is do our part. In my transition there was a very key former politician and current politician that played a significant role in advocating for me. I did not know the former personally, but GOD went before me and gave me favor with the person. Let me take a moment and show how this happened and I didn't even realize it was happening.

I was the Command Chief (Senior Enlisted Leader) of a military installation. I had worked previously with my boss, and so I hit the ground running finding places to add value and advance his objectives and goals when I joined him a second time. He was well respected in the community and had frequent engagements with the local leaders. Because of his respect for what I had previously done while under his command and what I was currently doing, unbeknownst to me, he was telling the local leaders how invaluable I was to him. He was telling them about what kind of a leader I was. He was championing me to them with no motive in mind other than to state how well we worked together as enlisted and officer and the value I added to him.

At the time I was not even thinking about my transition actively. I was busy taking care of people, taking care of the mission and advancing his objectives. At the time, he had no idea that I would stay in the local community and would seek employment. This took place for the next 12-15 months, unbeknownst to me. This was GOD going before me. Fast forward and as I am approaching retirement, one senior local leader in particular had conversations with me to ascertain if we were open to staying in the community. Now mind you, they do not ask every senior military leader to stay in their community. I was flattered, but still was clueless that this was GOD's favor going before me. Once I retired and made it known that we were going to stay local, GOD's favor kicked into overdrive. More advocacy from senior local leaders with whom I did not previously have a strong personal relationship. People sat down with me to give key advice and offer assistance. People of influence started to connect me to other people of influence. One meeting that stands out to this day was a former Command Chief at my installation connected me to a Chief Administrative Officer of a local municipality. I was blown away. It wasn't until the dust settled that I looked back and saw the full measure of favor that had gone before me.

So, I ask again, why not you?

10.

WHY NOT ME?

> "I DREAM OF PAINTING
> AND THEN I PAINT MY DREAM."
>
> -Vincent Van Gogh

SEED PLANTED

In February 2018, a big snowstorm shut down our community and most people were working from home. My boss and I were in the office. It was this day that I had the first conversation regarding city manager jobs. I was bored and needed some interaction, so I went to my boss' office and talked through a scenario with him. I compared the military base to a city and supposed him to be the mayor.

That being said, I asked him what he thought my position would equate to within the city. We looked at the leadership teams and positions for our surrounding areas and estimated that, depending on the size of the community, I could be a city manager, assistant city manager, in Human Resources or leading within the staff in some other way. It was a cool mental exercise for the moment, and back to work I went.

While attending a class three months later, I jokingly introduced myself as one who was going to be a city manager in the future. I didn't plan on saying that. It just fell out of my mouth. During a break, a classmate came to me and asked if I knew how to find those jobs, to which I said, "What jobs?" I forgot I had said, "City manager." He asked if I said city manager for clarity. Instead of admitting it was a joke, I said, "Yes." He mentioned that his best friend just got hired as a city manager, then gave me a link to search for job ads.

That evening I searched the website for the city manager positions. I found a few places that were very familiar to me, and I compared several locations. When I reflected on the responsibilities I had in previous years, the first thought, *Can I do this?* became a real question.

I started to have some doubts, then I saw enough variation in qualifications that would open the door for me. The combination of my previous jobs checked off many skills I saw listed as desired experiences. A few days went by, and I found myself clicking on the link again, examining more locations across the nation. What I discovered was that this may be something I could really do.

SEED GERMINATION

What I did next really catapulted me into a set of decisions that brought my future employment into reality. In August 2018, I spoke to a town manager with 33 years of experience, who was nearing retirement. I spent about an hour with him. I asked him if he would make an assessment about the potential of me becoming a city or town manager. I told him not to withhold anything, to give it to me straight. After the conversation, I was determined to follow this path.

At the end of our time together, the town manager informed me that I had relative experience but conveying it to others would be my challenge. We talked about things I needed to focus on in order to prepare for the transition. He gave me a few things to consider, and I started working on them the very next month. At that point I had less than two years from my intended transition into a new career.

The thought of being a city or town manager was prominent in every way from that point on. I set reminders in my phone to search for job postings, made meaningful connections, spoke with experienced people, took training classes, and other related tasks to enhance my understanding of the role I was pursuing.

You see, I really believed that GOD had implanted a thought in my heart and mind as to what my next career would be. I never imagined being a city or town manager before that random conversation in my boss's office. The encounter in the class provided me with a way to find open positions. I did not imagine what the adjustments looked like before spending time with the retiring town manager. Honestly, part of me perceived that this vision could be something I would have to work my way up to by serving in a subordinate position first. Regardless, I was convinced that GOD had implanted the idea into my heart. So, I had to come to a decision point. Should I go after what I believed to be GOD's leading, or go for something more attainable, easier, and familiar?

SEEDLING FORMS

I didn't totally abandon thoughts of other types of jobs, I just gave them very little attention. Subsequently, in December 2019, I had my first interview after six months of actively seeking and applying for openings. During the interview, the last question was asking why I applied for that location. It felt like a weird question. I wondered if they thought that I didn't qualify for some reason or if I was seen as a person just looking for a high paying job. Or even more challenging to me was, what if this was related to the previous question, where we talked about a portion of the underserved community. Was I seen as that? Based on my military background? It can't be. Or could it?

Too many thoughts ran through my head in a millisecond or more. My answer essentially, "Why not me?" I admitted that I almost didn't apply because of thoughts of starting at a lower position and growing towards a city or town manager position, but with what I have done and my capabilities I could adjust. Why not me?

Furthermore, I knew deep within that this was the path for me. What I didn't know was, was this the location for me? So, as I heard the question, I had to suppress all of the thoughts that flooded my mind. What was the angle for the question? Should I tell of the history of the town that I discovered? Do they think I can't handle it? Was my military service seen as being in a lower category of society, when compared to this community? Are they sending me a signal to back off? I had to relax and focus. And when I did, I was confident that this was what I was supposed to do. So, why not me?

It felt natural and terrifying at the same time. Could I be seen as arrogant, angry, disrespectful? The urge to downplay the moment crept in, but purpose pulled me forward. Starting my response with 'why not me' is what I did. I must admit, when I got in my truck and drove down the road, doubt came rushing in. *You fool, you blew it. You did so well until that.* To prevent being distracted while driving, I pulled over. After a while, reassurance came back to me. If this is the direction I am supposed to go in, I will know. If not, this is not the place for me. But I will not give up on the goal.

ADULT PLANT

Eight days later, the call came to set up a second round of interviews. After completing the final interview, I was called with confirmation of the town leaders' intent to hire me. What a blessing! Why not me?

Lessons Learned: Why not me? For real, why not me? What is your dream, passion, or next big idea? So, what are you going to do about it? Are you chasing it? When opportunities come before us, we either engage with enthusiasm and success, swing and miss, fall prey to self-doubt, or shy away altogether.

What we have to remember is this: allow GOD to lead and guide you. Chase the things that He ordains and designed for you. Recognize your purpose and resist the chances to give up or self-eliminate. Let GOD implant His desires into your heart, adopt them as your responsibility to steward His plans, and get after it. Doubt and fear will attempt to creep in, but you have to resist the urge to fight your own fire. There is enough of that out there. Be the first one to cheer on the champion within you.

When GOD has a plan for your life, don't back away from it. Step up, and step into it. You may have heard it said, "If GOD calls you to it, He will get you through it."

Why not you?

SIDEBAR #4:
DON'T LET YOUR FEELINGS FOOL YOU

After being in the position for a while, I decided to have a follow-up conversation with the person that asked me the final two questions from the interview mentioned. It turns out that the correlation and scenarios I formulated in my head had no linkage to the questioner's intent. I was all worked up in the moment, for what? Remember when I said I pulled over? I was cycling through how the conversation unfolded after I left the room. I had to calm down before driving home, especially since it was getting darker, and the roads were narrow. There's no room for error.

Question, how often do we psych ourselves out or allow an errant or random thought to push us to or over the edge? Had I taken a different approach, dipping into a negative connotation, I may be writing this portion with advice about how I acted upon unfounded assumptions. When I spoke with the person and mentioned the thoughts I had, we both realized how easy it is to have something taken out of context. One question had nothing to do with the next. Had I gotten in my feelings, in an outward way, I would have shut down the whole room, for no reason.

Feelings have their place, however, the negative thoughts we have proved to be distractions and self-defeating, if we give in to them. I challenge you not to fall prey to pre-exposures and historical engagements that were not pleasant. Call your future into reality, press past the pain and fears, so you can celebrate the next part of your destiny. Why not you? Stay focused!

11.

HOW BAD DO YOU WANT IT?

COMPLACENCY

Are you happy with where you are, or is there something threatening your current situation and demanding change? Reality will set you on a course of action. Have you ever watched or read the story of a music artist or actor that identified a deep struggle that they overcame? Maybe it was abject poverty or a jail sentence? Regardless, the person had a 'thing' that they never wanted to experience again. Too many of us do not have that measure of internal motivation. We are too comfortable. We may be dissatisfied, but not desperate to avoid an 'it.' Additionally, it is hard to work like you are hungry when your stomach is full.

At one point, after hearing the testimony of a music star, reality slapped me in the face. I never slept in my car, ate from a trash bin, or needed to avoid a return trip to jail. I could not have the same drive as those that did. But is there a way to manufacture the urgency or feeling? Not if you are overlooking the value and potential you bring to the table. You must remain authentic to yourself and find the inspiration that is applicable to you and your situation.

It wasn't until my final contract term was coming to a close that I had no choice but to engage things differently. I was too comfortable and content before that. I always had choices to make, until I didn't. What I mean is, I could simply renew the contract before. But I had reached the outer limits of the agreements. No more renewals, no extensions, no way to continue in the same way as before. So, what would I do next, and when? Am I prepared? What happens if I do not adjust in time?

Now I had a different outlook. It was time to get it in gear, I had to get my poop in a group for real.

I had to come to grips with the fact that I have a family with very specific needs. I know, who doesn't? Let me share a bit more. I have two adult children and two teens at the house, who my wife and I are developing into responsible adults (we hope). My youngest has a few health concerns. The type and levels of care needed is rather demanding. It took many years of care and prayer to find comfort in expecting this child to be awake the next morning. And there are chances that the future will require more interventions and therapies. My wife is the primary caretaker and non-medical attendant on a daily basis. I cannot allow the quality and access to care to go backwards for our family. This became my biggest motivation for a successful transition into a new career.

This is what keeps me honest about myself. What maintains my drive for achieving whatever is available? What scares me the most? Hmmm, I guess I don't have to manifest anything to inspire me after all. All of us have a uniquely important story in our lives, how are we using it to change our lives and future? What preventive measures do you need to take to establish or sustain provision through life's anticipated twists and turns?

WHAT IS YOUR TRUE DESIRE?

Do you have a strong desire for something to happen in your life? Do you put the right amount of effort and energy into acquiring or qualifying for it? Too often there is a mismatch in desire and action. Poor planning produces problematic products.

When I was younger, I watched the "Trials of Life" series, it was about various animals and their survival experiences. Whenever a hunt was on, it did not matter what else was happening, the animal seeking prey was laser focused on reducing the chance to miss a meal. Every step was careful, it often stayed low to the ground to avoid being seen, it tried not to make any startling or unnatural noise. It would stop and watch closely if there was an adverse reaction, or it would give it all it had to chase, capture, kill and consume the prey. Oh, but it started with identifying the right pattern and places to go.

Do you know where to go to find the prey, I mean, the career you want? Do you know what feeds the thing that you want to feed you? What are the milestones, education, accomplishments, and even the resting/hang-out spots for those in the profession? Are you able to endure the careful navigation through the sun, rain, thorns, and use the tall grass to your advantage? Are you skilled enough to avoid bringing adverse attention to yourself, when there are sticks and leaves everywhere you step? Knowing that your online and in-person presence may alert your prey before you get close enough to it. Can you identify when a hiring authority is uncomfortable or growing impatient, can you read the room well enough to adjust or strike at the most appropriate moment?

Do you have the energy, skill, and stamina for what you are chasing? Can you imagine a common household dog attempting to chase, capture, kill and consume an elephant - by itself? Or an alligator trying to hunt a cheetah? The outcome is largely dependent upon the environment. Even a lion may have trouble with a zebra if it gets caught by the hooves at the wrong time. My point is this, you have to know that you can take it—the chase, the encounter, the challenge once acquired, the help needed, the overall effort demanded for the prey you are chasing.

The same applies to the next career opportunity. How many people do you know that have landed a great job and they end up leaving relatively early? Is it possible that they looked at how big the opportunity appeared, and did not see the effort and energy required? Or maybe the environmental factors were not fully assessed.

DON'T CHASE A POSITION OR PENNY, SEEK PURPOSE & PASSIONS

It is vitally important for professionals in transition to see beyond the position or penny, it may be more appropriate to chase passion and purpose. When the focus is on what one may gain, as opposed to how one is to contribute, the experience is perceived and endured differently. The internal drive will indicate and direct how established our foundation is. Tenacity must exist to succeed. Besides, regardless of the type of career path, it will not always be easy. Can you stick to it when the comfort is not present, when the newness wears out?

Too many people give up before they prove to themselves that they have what it takes to excel in the field or position they landed. So, they take the easy way out, retreat to something familiar. Many military veterans default to the Department of Defense civil service jobs. Why not, it is a system they already know enough about. And for some that is the right move. That is what their purpose and passions drive them towards. I applaud those that do it for those reasons. But too many do it because, as stated previously, it is safe. It is comfortable. It is the easy button that does not require me to grow and stretch. And I get it, after putting a lot of effort to get to the point where you are in your career right now, you don't want to go through it again. To think about it makes you exhausted. I get it.

What I am fairly certain of is that voice deep down inside of you called "purpose" is not likely to be quiet nor satisfied. You may choose to try and ignore it and push it down and bury it, but it can't be silenced. How can I say that? I say that because it is very evident their voice is speaking because I hear people say things like, "Ah, man! Tomorrow is Monday, and I have to go back to work." Or they say, "Woohoo! It's hump day!" Or they say, "Thank GOD it's Friday!" When you are living according to purpose, according to why you were born into the earth, you don't see Mondays, hump-days and weekends. What you see is another day to get up and do what you do. What you see is another day to get up and make a difference. You see opportunity. You see purpose!

BEAST MODE

What is "beast mode"? Beast mode is elevating your game to a level where the average person can't even imagine. This is when you work so hard behind the scenes by getting up earlier and working longer to get better than your peers. This is when you have a fierceness in your eye that says, *I will not be defeated!* This is when you are so laser-focused that all you do is work on the fundamentals required to become the best. This is like Larry Bird shooting 500 free throws every day to become one of the best free throw shooters of all time. He was a beast.

It's like Kobe Bryant shooting the same shot over and over for over an hour to perfect it and then coming back the next day and doing the same thing. Was it any surprise that he was as good as he was? He told a story about how the average person gets in two workouts a day, but he decided he wanted to be the best, so he restructured his day and got in four workouts a day. Take four workouts a day and multiply that by years and you get a "compound interest" effect. This is beast mode.

Or how about Michael Jordan in the 90s? He was so committed to his craft. His work ethic was off the charts and his will to win was even higher. Not one, not two, not three NBA championships but six. And not only six but two sets of three-peats. That, my friend, is what we call "Beast Mode"!

Will we put in the work necessary to be able to switch into beast mode? What I can tell you about what you see on game day is that it does not originate on game day. Game day originates in the off-season. Gameday originates in practice. How hard do I train? How much film do I study? How hard do I analyze my game for areas of improvement year after year? Game day originates in going hard each and every practice no matter how long the season is. Game day originates by playing every practice as if it was the game.

This is what Jordan, Bryant, and Bird did. Are we willing to grind like we are hungry when we may not be hungry? Are we willing to put our pride down and approach the new endeavor as a "rookie" seeking to learn everything we can about the "league"? Are we willing to put aside things of comfort, like TV, video games, etc., in order to focus on the new craft in order to become one of the best? Are we willing to do what is necessary to become known in our new industry as Jordan was known in the 90's?

Can we switch into beast mode? Are we willing to switch into beast mode? What I know is that if you rose to the top rungs in your former career, you have the ability to go into beast mode. The question is, will you go into beast mode? Will you go hard in the paint, again?

12.

RUN THROUGH THE END

DOGGED PERSISTENCE

After you have made the decision to pursue
the new endeavor, you must continually conduct
your gap analysis. You have to constantly critique
yourself. What a lot of people don't know about the
sports heroes we revere is that, in their offseason,
they work with a coach to help them get better at
some aspect of their game. They do this every year,
even though they are the best of the best. Even
though they may have just won a championship,
they understand that they can always get better
and if they don't get better someone will sneak up
on them and overtake them.

They understand you are either growing or
atrophying. There is no such thing as maintaining.
As you pursue your new career, you must do
the same. This means proactively seeking input
from various trusted advisors, even when it
hurts, constantly. And once you get the input
you have to continue to prep (do the work). Take
the classes. Read the books. Work on public
speaking. Work on your written communication.

We must continue to do the work. The prep is everything! Stephen Keague is quoted as saying, "Proper planning and preparation prevents poor performance." HH says it this way, "Poor planning produces problematic products."

GOAL IN SIGHT

We must start prepping for the interview. How, you ask? I'm glad you asked. Talk to people in the field you desire to transition. Ask them to give you a mock interview. This does not have to be someone local. This can be someone at a distance that you conduct a mock phone interview with or a video conference interview. But if you have a company in your local area within a reasonable drive, I encourage you to call them up and ask if they would give you a mock interview. You never know, if you have been in Beast Mode, they might be so impressed that they may become interested in hiring you. Even if not, you will gain some valuable insight on how you can get better. Continue to prep anyway.

Another way to prepare for the interview is to use internet searches. Put in something like, "What are the top interview questions in the civil engineer industry?" or "What are the most common interview questions for an executive?" You will be amazed at the resources you can find by putting the right request into the search bar.

As stated previously, prep for me began July 29, 2017, and my first interview was September 6, 2017. I had prepped so hard, and I was definitely in beast mode. I had studied their website. I studied their SWOT analysis. I read every single document I could get my hands on multiple times, and I spoke to every person who would talk to me about the organization. I read through the documents over and over and highlighted what I thought was key information and from the things I highlighted I dug for additional information, which led me to dig for more information until I had exhausted the information I could find.

I approached it as if I was going to give a mission brief on a critical mission like when I was in the military. When I wore the uniform, when given a task, I left no stone unturned as I did not want to show up ill prepared. I would stay up late the night prior rehearsing and rehearsing to make sure I knew my content so well that even if there was a problem with the audio/video system, I could brief my content from memory as I passed out paper copies. The bottom line was that while in the military I took my preparation very seriously and if I wanted to be successful in this transition, I needed to do the same. So that is what I did. I got to know the material by heart as I would not be giving a PowerPoint presentation, I would be answering random questions on the fly.

I deliberately thought about questions they might ask me, and I gave a lot of thought and rehearsed my answers over and over again. I got my wife to play the interviewer and give me feedback. I recorded myself, while giving responses to potential questions and then I would critique myself. I did not watch a lot of TV or do things for entertainment during this time. I was laser-focused on my prep work and completing my graduate degree which I knew would increase my chances of landing the position.

Oh, by the way, the year prior to my transition (I had a hard stop at 30 years), I was working on my master's degree after just completing my undergraduate degree, while in the most demanding job of my life and I was fully engaged in my role and duties. One might not have known I was close to retirement as hard as I worked. What's my point, I didn't shortchange my job in my transition. In the military we call this being Retired on Active Duty (R.O.A.D.).

SIDEBAR #5:
IT'S NEVER TOO LATE

I hope you caught that I did not complete all of the requirements for my undergraduate degree until I was 28 ½ years into a 30-year career. It was very tough, but I completed all of the requirements to graduate with my graduate degree prior to leaving active duty. The point is not to pat myself on the back. The point is to encourage you that it's never too late to pursue your dreams no matter what they are. Go after that degree. Go after that career. Don't let anything hold you back. Truthfully, the only thing that can hold you back is You. You got this, so go get it! Also don't wait so late in your career to complete your education.

GAME TIME

I was not jogging as I approached my new opportunity, I was running. When it came to interview day I was up early. I had picked out my suit and tie the night prior. I had a fresh haircut. My shoes were clean and polished. I ate a good breakfast. I ran through some more mock interview questions to make sure my responses were sound. I read back through all of the documents I had gathered over the previous months. I was ready!

Did I tell you the first interview was a phone interview? Why would I do all of this for a phone interview, where no one would be able to see me? I was going "Jordan in the 90's." I was approaching the situation as if I might not get another chance and by prepping the night before and getting dressed the day of, I was switching my mindset into "Beast Mode." The night Kobe hit 60 points against Toronto, he wasn't thinking about how many shots he made. He was in beast mode and was just in the zone.

That is what I planned to do once the interview commenced. I was going to be in the zone. This led to being invited for a second in-person interview. One might think that since I had been prepping for this long and the first interview went well that I would stop prepping and relax or maybe throttle back a little. That is not what I did. I took it up a notch. I spent more time in the days leading up to the interview reading over the same material I had read previously to see if there was something else for me to glean or if there was something I missed.

What I knew was when given the opportunity, I was not going to miss the shot due to a lack of preparation. I was going to be like Larry Bird on the free throw line in game seven with zero seconds left on the clock and we are 1 point behind. I was going to be like Jordan in 1982 when he hit the game winning shot to give the Tarheels the victory in the NCAA championship game in the final seconds. I was going to go hard in the paint. I had prepped hard. I was ready and I hit the shot. I was selected for the position. Mostly due to GOD's grace, mercy, and favor. The other part was hard work as faith requires work to materialize. The great Muhammad Ali famously said, "The fight is won or lost far away from witnesses – behind the lines, in the gym, and out there on the road, long before I dance under those lights."[11] I had put in the work.

SIDEBAR #6:
DON'T HAVE TO SPRINT THE ENTIRE RACE

Man, that guy was running hard! I encourage everyone to avoid having to do that type of sprint. I know, because I also had to run through the end, regarding education. You see, I had a complete degree, but it was not in business. Remember when I mentioned that I started trying to close the gaps the month after I talked with the experienced town manager? I started a second bachelor's degree and not simply go after the master's degree. I felt I needed to get the financial background and then seek the graduate degree. This meant that I could not finish before I hit my 30-year mark in the Air Force. In fact, it meant I had to double up on classes, while in a very busy position, where I really did not own all of my time.

I actually had two plans for education. I had a good understanding of the qualifying degree types to consider and could not acquire a public administration degree at the MA level, so I decided to seek the business administration BA and then switch to a different degree at a certain point. Why? Because a done degree is a done degree. I needed some very purposeful classes, my assessment, and I would find them in business admin. So, I front-loaded those courses. I informed my counselor in the first few conversations that I would likely switch at the marketing class. And that is what happened. The program I completed was much faster overall, my purpose was accomplished with the financial courses and there was more work to do!

Can you imagine racing a clock to qualify for a job opportunity, getting the job before finishing the degree, then continuing on the previous pace to finish the degree with no breaks? After getting hired, I considered slowing down the aggressive class schedule, but I didn't. Learning the new job, new community and leading a team that serves almost 19,000 people every day, while taking two classes per session was less than fun. But it was needed, the real truth is, it could have been avoided. Had I started the program three or six years ago, or finished the program I started in 2008, I would not have been as stressed. Oh yeah, I did not mention the global pandemic was just catching traction when I started in the new position. I did not apply the principle of "if you stay ready, you won't have to get ready" related to my education.

For those not at the point of transition, remember this, a done degree is a done degree. Get something completed! If your life is busy now, how much busier will it be when you are changing careers, moving, finding a house, learning a new team, getting familiar with the new area, making friends, setting up school for kids, etc. If you have an inkling of what degree to earn, do it. I wasted time, it did not hinder my current opportunity, but I searched for six months before getting the first interview. Could it have been a distraction? It won't be that way again for me. I have applied for a school regarding the Master of Public Administration, one month after completing the certification program I was told about years ago. My goal is to finish before my current contract is finished.

If you know the education requirements of the industry that you believe you will go into, then go ahead and get that degree. Look at several job advertisements, compare, and decide. Does the school's name matter? Not that I can see, unless it is an ivy league school. Other than that, just get it done. I chose to complete the second bachelor's degree, then a certificate program, and now back to the Master program. Subsequent to that, I may accomplish a credentialed manager program with the largest association I am aware of in municipal management. All of these actions will make me more marketable, but more importantly, more effective.

Too many people think they can ride into the sunset with the previous experience as their most marketable skill. No problem if you have a transferable skill, with the appropriate terminology and credentials. Otherwise, you need to do what is necessary to get past the electronic screener. The electronic screener is the computer program that will review and score your resume. This system has no emotions and cannot be influenced in that way. Know the arena you are going into, make the adjustments, then run through the finish line.

13.

BUILD THE NEXT TEAM OF CHAMPIONS

Once you have triumphantly transitioned into your new role or career, the work does not stop there. If you and I both stop and reflect, we will see that we did not arrive at where we are on our own. We had numerous people along the path helping us. Some of them were there for the entire journey, some for part of the journey and some for only a brief moment but all of them are woven into the tapestry of your journey and each one, no matter how small a role they played, were an important part of your triumphant transition.

Now it is our turn to pay it forward. Whether it is someone in your company or your family or from the gym where you work out or via someone reaching out on LinkedIn, all of us will encounter someone either thinking about transitioning or in the process of transitioning. I believe we owe it to the "system" to pay back at a minimum, what we received, but in order to sustain the "system" long term, we should deposit more than we received and leave it better than when we found it.

How do we do this? Be open and available. If someone reaches out, make time to meet with them virtually or at a local coffee shop. Be available to speak to groups and be open about your fears and challenges, in addition to your successes. Talk openly and frequently about what the process was like for you. Your story will encourage and inspire others to either start or continue their process. There is a statement that iron sharpens iron. Someone may need you to sharpen them by being a sounding board or by pushing back on false assumptions. We must freely share all of the information we received with others and do all we can to help them be successful.

We can either be a river or a reservoir. A river flows freely, the water stays fresh, and it gives life to many humans, plant life, and animals. A reservoir starts out fresh and life giving, but it keeps all of its water. It neither gives, nor is it refreshed. And over time, what starts out as life giving, spoils. It becomes stagnant and bacteria starts to grow, and the once life-giving source becomes a hazard.

I'll put it a different way. If I have $100 in my hand, with my hand open, what can you take from me? Answer: Everything. What can you give me? Answer: Everything. The money can be multiplied as it is put to use. If I have $100 in my hand and my hand is clenched, what can you take from me? Answer: Nothing. What can you give me? Answer: Nothing. Be a giver and sow into the lives of others. Build tomorrow's champions!

As we build tomorrow's champions for a triumphant transition, we not only are of service to them, but we are also of service to ourselves. As we share and recount the stories to others, we are reinforcing lessons learned and many times gleaning new lessons and skills that can be used when our next transitions come, as life is full of transitions, seen and unseen. Through the process of helping others, we live out the maxim: If you stay ready, you'll be ready!

14.

FOR STUDENTS
(High School, Trade Schools & Post-Secondary)

SHORT OR LONG RUNWAY, YOU DECIDE

I graduated high school in 1987, and unfortunately, I don't think much has changed with regard to freshmen beginning their first day with the end in mind. My first day of high school, I was laser focused on how I was dressed and if I would impress the girls. I wanted to continue with my reputation of being a cool jock. Thinking about transitioning in four years was nowhere on my mind. If you had mentioned something like that to me, I probably would have looked at you like you were speaking a foreign language. Yet, if you want to be successful in your transition to the college of your desires or the career of your dreams, having this mindset is essential.

What do I mean? If every freshman approached their first day thinking more about what their transition will be in four years, they would approach their studies differently. They may cultivate different habits and more than likely adjust the company they keep. When this is not the approach, you may find yourself looking like me. I was an exceptionally smart kid with average grades. My SAT scores were average. Being completely honest with myself and my athletic ability, I was average at best. From school to athletics, I had not applied myself to the degree I could have in preparation for the inevitable transition in four years.

I liked to party and chase girls. I liked to party so much that drinking the night before a football game became normal. What serious athlete does that? I did not begin with the end in mind. I knew a Trigonometry test was coming up and despite knowing that I was not prepared, I still did not seek after school assistance from my teacher. So, was it a surprise when I was a senior, that I had a 3.2 GPA with no scholarship offers in my mailbox? In actuality, it was for me. That is how ignorant I was to the process. It should have been of no surprise. I reaped the end I had in mind. I was a cool jock that was popular with the girls and could hold his own drinking. This did not enable my dreams of grandeur of being a highly sought-after college football player.

AGRICULTURAL APPROACH

When you begin with the end in mind everything you do should be approached knowing that you are a novice, and you need to become really good by the time your transition (graduation) approaches. Everything you do from homework assignments to research papers to sports practice must be approached with the goal of becoming the best version of you possible. You want to be a subject matter expert (SME) for your level.

If this is your approach, then you understand that a seed planted does not sprout up overnight.

Let's think about this from an agricultural viewpoint. A farmer knows that if a certain product is desired, the combination of efforts must be concentrated towards the needs of that crop. The seed, soil, environment, fertilizer, even knowing what would destroy or hinder the growth process. The timing of harvest is considered relative to the planting and tending to the process.

So, your process should include determining

what you hope to have as a harvest. Do you know what you want to do or become later? What does it take to get there, from an educational standpoint? Are there experiences you can plan to gain along the way? How close are professionals in that field? Oh wait, even if there are no experts in your local area, use the internet and social platforms to build you, instead of only entertaining you.

Establishing meaningful relationships and deepening your interpersonal communication skills is critically important. The earlier you start on this, the better. Volunteering in line with your future goals is a superb way to build experience and credibility. Not only that, but you just might also find yourself gaining a mentor, or even better, a sponsor. A mentor will facilitate your learning process, but a sponsor may speak on your behalf, and help you walk into rooms or conversations that would normally be closed to you.

It boils down to crafting, or cultivating, your chances to reap a harvest that can feed your future. Think about it, the harvest is the career of choice. How do you get there? What seeds or foundational input do you need? Are you willing to do what it takes to get into, to be in, or stay in the right environments and crowds? What is your level of commitment? Can you recognize those things and places that may hinder the harvest you expect?

Just like the farmer, you have to know that the process must run its course properly. Taking shortcuts may not produce what is most beneficial as an outcome. Similar to agriculture, acceleration by artificial means could introduce health hazards in the long run. Attempting to sidestep some of the smaller tasks, you know, the ones that are not so exciting, are actually character building. I remember a time when I had some extra responsibilities that I did not like or appreciate real time, but the truth proved that those experiences gained in that period of time fueled successes later in my career and life. I literally became thankful for the very things I dreaded earlier. Do your best to avoid skipping meaningful and foundational opportunities. Success should be escorted by meaningful experiential knowledge, even when those times are not as fun as you may imagine. Stay with it and cultivate your future properly.

LEARN TO LEAD,
NOT JUST MARK BUBBLES

Who likes to take tests? That's a real question. I know there are some of you that enjoy tests, but the deeper work is the preparation. Subsequently, we have the test results. The grade is a partial indication of the learning process, but is it the end of the growth process? Does it prove that success awaits?

I submit that the real test begins when you are in the workforce. But if you believe that your education is supposed to fuel your future, why is cramming, and dumping such a prevalent part of so many students' test prep strategy? If you have done this, I urge you to stop it immediately. If you see schooling as an irrelevant part of a system built to exchange money for certificates and degrees, then do what you feel is appropriate for now, but know that you are short-changing yourself and the future depth of knowledge that could be gained.

If every student endeavored to study for the

sake of application, instead of just providing an answer to a test, we just might build subject matter experts and greater leaders earlier in life. Why not utilize your school research, writing and projects to invite your future into your present? Can you imagine, your teacher, or professor, asking you why you took the angle on your assignment and your response indicates true applicability to real life and not just theory? Could that illuminate to them the measure of seriousness within you? Who knows if that could open doors for you? In fact, this kind of focus and intentional effort has sparked professional faculty members to conduct outreach in order to help a dedicated student keep their fire burning.

Again, from this point on, if you have been cramming and dumping, stop doing that immediately. Invest whole-heartedly in your future by learning and studying for the sake of advancing your opportunities for your dreams and aspirations. Marking bubbles are for grades, if you limit your educational experience to that, does that potentially equate to limits later in life? It all depends on you. I encourage you to approach each assignment and research paper as an opportunity to become the subject matter expert that awaits deep inside of you. This is an opportunity to add some tools to your toolkit.

BUILD YOUR RESUME NOW

This section will dovetail off the previous two sections. Are we starting with the end in mind? Whether we are preparing to apply to college or enter the workplace, we must begin with the end in mind in this area too. If we understand that each assignment is an opportunity to become a subject matter expert, it would behoove us to understand that we have ample opportunity to build our resume now.

Are we a good follower? Do we add value to others? Can we be trusted? Can we lead? These are questions colleges and employers alike want to know and we can definitely answer them all through volunteerism. Volunteering provides a tremendous opportunity to add value in our communities and build critical skill sets. From the Girl Scouts to your local church to the local soup kitchen, from the Parent Teacher Association to the community garden to the non-profit that runs an afterschool reading program, there are numerous places to add value.

As we take time to help the various entities to execute their mission, along with our service comes a strong sense of fulfillment that we experience, as it is always better to give than to receive. This may be the biggest benefit from giving our time and efforts to others.

In addition, as a tertiary impact, we gain and/or hone skills. How? Glad you asked! There will be a need for money management. If we are skilled in this area, we take advantage of an opportunity to highlight our prowess. Can you identify inefficiencies or shortfalls in a process and then make the process better? If so, this adds to your resume. There will inevitably be opportunities to lead a project or event. Will we step up and lead? Can we organize things so that the events flow smoothly? Are we able to raise funds to execute an event? Are we able to effectively bring together a group of volunteers under one purpose? If so, this all adds to our resume in ways to translate those 'soft skills' that leaders and managers talk about.

SIDEBAR #7:
LEADING VOLUNTEERS EXPANDS YOUR
LEADERSHIP EFFECTIVENESS

I want to take a moment to slow down. After 30 years in the United States Air Force and four years of leadership at the local government level, one thing that I know for a fact that is a key indicator of leadership skill is one's competence in leading a group of volunteers. Volunteers have a choice that they can exercise at any moment. If we don't treat them well, lead them well or we are unorganized, they won't follow us, and the project will fail or have poor execution. If you want to build your leadership skills, spend time in this area. Take time to get some honest feedback from the folks you led and work to improve.

When applying to college, the administrators want to know if they are admitting a "whole" person. What does this mean? Translation: Does the application show he is more than just a smart person? Does the application show that he will be a good fit into the school's culture? Does that application indicate he aligns with the school's core values? There are hundreds of thousands of students applying to college with good grades. How will this student differentiate himself? Serving others may possibly be the answer if he desires to be competitive.

Now with that said, it is not just about volunteering once or twice. Consistency matters. It is about sustained superior performance, with emphasis on sustained. So, if we start with the end in mind, then each year we will intentionally decide which clubs or agencies we will volunteer for and how often we will volunteer. Yes, I am saying plan out the year. It may change and we may have to subtract some events or maybe we will decide to add some, but the point is to develop a plan and then work the plan.

As you volunteer, you need to keep track of your activities, otherwise, you will not remember a lot of the small details when it is time to fill out applications. Be sure to track the five "W's," three "H's" and the "I."

THE FIVE "W'S"

Who – Who did you volunteer for?

What – What was the event, what did you do?

Where – Where was this? Where there any unique aspects or challenges to overcome?

When – Is there an aspect of timing to highlight that makes this notable or special?

Why – Why was it necessary to have the event?

These questions should be easily answered by someone within the organization.

THE THREE "H'S"

How many people were involved/led/impacted?
How much money was involved?
How did you overcome challenges?

"I" IS FOR IMPACT

What was the impact of the event?
Who was impacted by the event?
Why should I care that you did what you did?
How did what you did make a difference?
What was enhanced, mitigated, or prevented?

If we can be consistent and track our activities, we can build an extremely strong resume. Before we transition, I want to reemphasize there are clear benefits for you by volunteering, but the greatest gift will be what you feel internally when you serve others. Your heart will swell.

SIDEBAR #8:
DELIBERATELY TRACK YOUR EFFORTS

By tracking this information, it will prepare you for S.T.A.R. questions or statements during the interview process. If you do not know what these are, I encourage you to look it up. This information captures the data for use in the future to tell a full, complete, and compelling story that could make the difference in being hired or not.

I have sat across from multiple candidates who have had resumes that sing like a world-famous opera singer, but when I looked them in the eye and asked them to give me an example, many looked at me like a deer looking into headlights. In all but one case, I did not select the individuals with a poor response. Do the work and capture the data, save it, and review it periodically. If you stay ready, you'll be ready!

SUBSTANCE FUELS CHOICE

I had the honor of sitting as a panel member for the state selection to attend military service academies. What I will share here will hopefully inspire you to be proactive in your activity choices throughout the education portion of your career, even in high school. As the team reviewed the myriad of applications, each of us had independent viewpoints and passion areas. We received some guidance from the process owner and established our methods for scoring the records. Notice that I did not say individuals. The people did not come into an interview as a first step. Their records were our introduction to the person, much like one's cover letter and resume.

There are many factors to consider, so my goal is not to give you the keys to the kingdom by stating this trait or experience is better than another, rather, I intend to show you that there is value to your participation in events, organizations, and initiatives. Equally important is the way you capture those activities on paper.

Let's play a quick game. I have a few cups, each one is different in content, but the same in design. One cup is empty. The second cup has water only. Next is water and ice, and then one with juice, followed by one with southern style sweet tea. Yet another has soda on ice. Which one would you choose, and why? There is nothing fundamentally wrong with any of the choices, depending on what you want or need at the time, your selection will be made.

The empty cup has the opportunity to add whatever one has already or improves the capability to wait for the option most craved. The others are largely based on preference, or an assessment of benefit anticipated. Each cup, if it could speak, would say 'pick me' but it is not in control of being picked. The consumer, or hiring manager, would likely balance the needs, advertised criteria and how the beverage would 'fit' with the rest of the meal (employed staff). So, it comes down to the question of, do you have what is being sought for the situation and meal?

If you know some preferences of the choosers, why wouldn't you attempt to find a match that you would fit into as well as their desire to find someone for the company? Imagine yourself as a cup of freshly squeezed organic juice, the likelihood of you being picked for a high calorie, overt fat content meal would seem disjointed and incongruent. Even if you were picked, others may wonder why you were there, causing some measure of discomfort for many involved, including you. Oh, but it feels great to be chosen, right? How much better is it to fit in and be useful?

But I get it. You can change, right? In order to fit in, no! You are unable to change the chemical composition of who you are. Juice will not become soda or any other substance. Attempting to do this miracle change could manifest confusion and frustration. Many people make the mistake of selling the statement that they can change. The employers that take a chance on the juice that thinks they will become soda are extending grace and mercy, knowing the chemical transformation will not fully manifest. Eventually, one of the two will face reality. Do not over promise something just to fit in. Every rejection is not a detriment, some of them are redirection back to your true self.

SIDEBAR #9:
SQUARE PEG IN A ROUND HOLE

I had a critically important position to fill once, and I was very deliberate to sit down with my team to craft specific requirements (chemical consistency) for the position. After going through the process, it was narrowed down to three candidates. Two eliminated themselves and the third was a very strong candidate but they did not have one of the critical elements. It was clear from their resume and from the interview that they were missing this item. They made a strong attempt to show that they could change. I knew in my gut that the missing factor would make the job difficult for them, but I ignored my gut and gave them the space and grace to attempt to change who they were.

Things started off great, but within a short while the one critical element that they did not have became a problem and remained a problem until things became untenable. We both were frustrated and no matter how hard they tried; they could not change their chemical composition.

And it wasn't that they were a bad person, they were just not the right person for this particular position. Eventually, the person was terminated.

Don't try to make yourself fit in. Find where you fit and become the best candidate you can be.

Here are some things you could be doing while in school. These types of ideas may help build your files that will be evaluated later by others. Doing these things might increase the perceptions of you being a leader or identify viable potential in a given field of work:

• **Join or create committees along the way,** don't just be on the roll, set out to lead people and teams as well as have some measure of budget oversight, even if it is $723. The dollar amount may not be large, but it shows accountability for other people's money, and lends itself for assessing trustworthiness. Examine how the position qualifications for the career you want aligns with the organization and volunteer in those areas to build relatable and transferable experiences and skills.

• **Task management and time management principles should be on display in your file.** This will help you in many ways, as there are very few job sectors where one would only focus on a single process without additional workloads or responsibilities.

• **Be bold enough to get involved in city and school community organizations.** This will often be attributed to maturity and focus beyond personal gain. It also connects you with people with broader thought processes and relationships.

• **Show you can add value beyond personal ambitions.** You may be surprised with the wisdom you gain in an activity where your focus is on other people and the betterment for a wider audience.

SEEKING ADVICE

We should seek advice from people in roles you desire, not just from people you know or who look like you. What do I mean? We all belong to communities. Communities help us to feel safe and loved. The challenge may arise when there is no one in our community that is employed or has any experience in our desired profession.

When there is no one in your community that can help guide you, you have to get outside of your comfort zone and seek advice and input from somewhere else. Even if there are people in your community that can give you advice, I encourage you to seek out multiple credible voices to help guide you. I want to emphasize, credible. Remember, there may be people in your community who can connect you to the right people.

NEW JOB APPLICANTS

As hiring agents, we have seen some terrible applications and resumes. Some were so poorly constructed that it was truly taxing to digest the information. Some people became minimalists, which prevented opportunities to understand or evaluate what responsibilities or impacts were satisfied. Unfortunately, there have been a few submissions that were unprofessional in appearance.

Some thoughts on things to avoid:

• Do not send handwritten files or typed products with written adjustments marked on the pages.

• Stains on printed products are not acceptable while seeking a job.

• Be careful about being too fancy, unless it is appropriate for the industry you are seeking to enter. Fancy font choices may not be as easy to read as you might think, what happens if the reviewer has sight impairments that are impacted by the creative script choices you made? Do you think the risk is worth it?

• Failing to properly label an email or file could cause unexpected delays. If you send an email to a business with a one- or two-word subject line, your message may be overlooked or perceived as a solicitation note. Consider adding the job ad number and position title to the email and files, this tells them up front what subject they are engaging.

• Don't think people will know what you intended, write in ways that leave the reader no ambiguity.

In some instances, we have seen some great files, but the interview was disappointing. Do yourself a favor. Regardless of the amount of confidence you have that you received a call for an interview, prepare for the interview. Planning to just wing it may produce awkward and distracting moments. Chances are, this would not be good for you. If possible, seek out mock or informational interviews.

15.

FOR MILITARY & VETERANS

This section is written to speak specifically to those who are serving or have served the nation in uniform. It may apply to other industries, but the intent is to speak to some of the things we do specifically that hinder us from having a triumphant transition. However, you can keep reading if you are not a veteran!

A. ITS HARD TO WATCH PEERS' PROGRESS.

This is not the case for everyone, but it definitely was for me. As I approached 30 years, I felt I was just really getting into my groove, and I had a lot more in the tank to give. I was enjoying serving and wanted to continue to serve. Weekly in my mind, I would run through scenarios that might allow me to serve beyond 30. I was not ready to stop. Then I saw peers of mine moving on to the next level, which was proof positive that I too could have served at the next level if given the opportunity and I felt I would have made a difference. Truthfully, it was tough to watch my peers move on as I was exiting the service. For a period of time, I took a hiatus from social media, because I didn't want to see the announcements of my peers moving on to higher responsibilities. I know that is shallow and selfish, but that is where I was at. Thankfully, I had a new career opportunity to keep me looking forward and my wife very lovingly kept encouraging me to look forward. If it were not for my wife and a fantastic opportunity, I can see how I could have fallen into a depression. It was very easy for me to get lost in my head thinking about what could have been if I had continued to serve.

What I began to see over time, not overnight, was that if I would have continued to serve, I would not have been able to take advantage of this opportunity that is not afforded to many enlisted people. Because of the words of my previous two bosses, the community knew I was an impact player and they had gotten a chance to know me. Fortunately, they felt a connection and wanted me to stay in the local area. If I would have moved to another base, I would not have been at the wing level and therefore would not have had as much contact with the local community and may not have had the exposure to the key players in the local community which helped to facilitate my successful transition.

I mean to say that I had some very influential people in the community advocating on my behalf and I will be forever grateful. So, when it comes time for you to move on, hopefully you don't have my struggle, but if you do, find something to focus on that forces you to look out the windshield versus the rearview mirror.

B. WE LET THE UNIFORM, RANK OR TITLE BECOME WHO WE ARE.

There is a lot of respect that comes along with serving in the armed forces and as we progress in rank, additional respect comes. With each promotion, there usually is a commensurate amount of power comes with the rank. Whether we choose to admit it or not, power can be addictive and cause us to want to remain in power, which in turn means we can start to become our uniform or rank. You have met the individuals. They are retired but they still want you to refer to them by their retired rank. Or they are retired, and it seems like they forgot they retired by how they engage, especially when on a military installation. The regulations have changed, unbeknownst to them, but they spout off your discrepancy in accordance with what they last remember, and they do it with such disdain despite the fact they are wrong. This perspective can often cause us to treat our pending transition as if it is a figment of our imagination and leave us and our families ill prepared.

C. WE DON'T INCLUDE OUR SPOUSE IN THE CONVERSATION, OR WE DO IT TOO LATE.

How many of you have gotten the response of "I support you" in a conversation about a career impacting decision? How did that make you feel? Confirmed? Empowered? Loved?

I challenge you to never take that as an answer again. It authorizes your loved one to subordinate and silence how they really feel. That is not fair, and it is not what you really want or need.

I realized this some years after making a

decision that my wife was not thrilled with. At the time, she gave me the support response as a closing comment. For whatever reason, we were talking about the past and she admitted that she wasn't thrilled about that action back then but knew how much I wanted it. I laughed and said I wasn't that excited, but she said, "Sure, I support you." So, we did it. Can you imagine how many times this happens in life? Neither one of us was excited, both of us thought the other was good, and later we regretted it all. This could have been avoided if we had a full, unimpeded conversation.

If we approach too passionately or too late, it tends to stifle a real discussion. Is that what we want? Transitions are critical times in life, and the impacts could last for decades. If this is rushed or abbreviated unnecessarily, disappointment may rush in later. It may be uncomfortable, or seem to be out of control, but it must be done. Had I not accepted "I support you," we could have saved a lot of money and hardships.

The adage of "two are better than one" holds true. When you have a loved one in your life, keeping the relationship on one accord is even more special when major changes are upon you.

D. WE THINK THERE IS AN EXCEPTION TO THE RULE. WE THINK WHEN WE PULL OUR HAND OUT OF THE WATER THERE WILL BE A HOLE. WE WILL STILL BE NEEDED.

As we ascend to the top ranks in the military, there is a lot of satisfaction of being involved in making people's lives better and getting the mission done. We start to feel like we are an integral part of the process and rightfully so, because we are heavily involved. But the bottom line is that our system is designed so that once we have made the decision to retire, there is someone being designated in the system to replace us. It does not matter how great or effective we were. It does not matter how many great things we did.

Once we are a week or so out from our retirement ceremony, there is someone who has shown up or will be showing up to take our place. Why do I point out the obvious? Because we fail to do the necessary prep-work to make a successful transition. For some reason, we act like we will not be replaced. We put our head down and focus on the mission all the way up to the day of our ceremony, which is commendable. But this is not very effective in creating a smooth transition for you and your family. When you pull your hand out of the water, the water is no longer displaced. It automatically fills in the hole you once created.

E. WE DON'T OPENLY TALK TO OTHERS IN UNIFORM WHO WE TRUST ABOUT OUR FEARS.

As a result of having had some negative encounters with some of my peers about my dreams and goals post-military in the very beginning, I was afraid to talk openly about my fears. I did have one military brother in the local community who had done something similar to what I was endeavoring to do and again, I thank GOD for my bride. She kept me grounded, but I did not want to take all of my fears to her because she had concerns about the transition too. I needed to be her rock, so it would have been great to have some of my local peers available to use as a sounding board. And to be fair, I am sure there were some that would have been supportive, but I did not give the chance. My perspective was once burned twice shy. I should have opened up. Don't repeat my mistake.

F. WE DON'T TAKE THE TAP (TRANSITION ASSISTANCE PROGRAM), EXECUTIVE TAP, OR CHIEF'S TAP SERIOUSLY.

I have heard many stories about folks saying I don't need to go to TAP, I'm good or they sign up for TAP and then they do not prioritize TAP and allow the call of duty to pull them out of the class and thereby not get the full intended impact of the class. I don't understand this thought process. If you are a career service member, or if you have served for a four year commitment, the chances are that you have not done this before and can use all the help you can get to make it a triumphant transition. I think the flippant attitude towards TAP leads to people ending up in jobs where they are less than satisfied, which leads to job hopping trying to scratch that "itch" or they don't feel they get hired for the types of positions they feel they are qualified for. Over time this can lead to greater frustration, withdrawal and even depression. Whatever your job was in the military, you enjoyed making a difference, in most cases, and you enjoyed being good at what you did. Not having that feeling can cause psychological impacts.

TAP, Executive TAP, and Chief's TAP exist to help us transition successfully. Are they perfect? No, they are not. But they absolutely give us a leg up at something we likely have never done before. We have to take it seriously. I remember the first time I went to Executive TAP, I was about four years out from my 30-year mark. It was a great class, but I was not focused. My head was still in my current role and where I thought I might transition next. The only smart thing I did was I kept all of my notes and binders from the class. They proved to be a great resource to me later as I was crafting my resume and honing my elevator pitch.

I went to Chief's TAP at year 29 and I was fully focused. It reminded me of things from my previous class and added some new tools to my toolkit. After the class, I followed up with the instructor for feedback a couple of times. Then I attended a local TAP course at my base. Even though I had been through two higher level courses, I found value in attending this: (1) It reminded me that this transition was real, and I needed to take it seriously; (2) It gave me a chance to have my resume reviewed by a different set of eyes and practice interviewing; (3) Many points made during the other classes were reinforced.

The bottom-line was, I was better prepared for a transition to something completely new. All of my adult working life had been spent in the United States Air Force and I was now going into a world that spoke a completely different language and had many different operating procedures. Whether I wanted to admit it or not, I needed some help.

G. WE DON'T PUSH OUTSIDE OF OUR COMFORT ZONE, WHEN IT COMES TO NETWORKING TO GET A JOB BECAUSE IT SEEMS WEIRD.

I remember very clearly, the thought of calling a stranger to ask for a "hook up" to meet someone of influence who might be able to open a door for me was just plain weird. The thought of it made me shudder. After I retired, when I was out in the community and even to this day, all around me, it is commonplace for people to ask for a business card and then cold call you the following week. For them it is nothing. For me it was not only weird at first, but rude. I had never had to do this in my entire adult life and now at the age of almost 49 I needed to do this? I was paralyzed at first. HH was much better at this than me. I slowly inched out into the water and thanks to some key folks in my local community, it became less weird for me. They helped me by introducing me to people, which led to other conversations. This was way outside of my comfort zone, but it was necessary. What I know now and see is, people who do this are supremely confident that either they can add value to you, or you can add value to them. We have to get over ourselves.

H. WE DON'T WANT TO PAY TO GET HELP.

I don't know, but many military members below the rank of flag officer (General) hesitate and even flail against paying someone for a service that will help them transition. Maybe it is because over the course of our careers we have had to improvise and figure it out to ensure mission success. If you do not listen to anything else, please listen to this. If you are not good at writing, pay good money to a credible company to help translate all of the great things you did into a language that the new industry will understand. One thing that I took great pride in was when I received feedback that my resume was easy to read and understand and it was very helpful that I related my past experiences to the job I was applying for in the resume. Yes, it was a targeted resume and not a general resume. The money you invest will be well worth the time you save banging your head against the wall each time you do not make it through the initial gate when applying for opportunities. And once you have a solid general resume, you may be able to modify it on your own for specific opportunities, but if not make the investment in yourself. If you are going to bet on anyone or anything, bet on yourself.

16.

SECRET
SAUCE

This next section of the book will speak to Christian faith principles. If you are not of the Christian faith or take offense to the Christian faith, we respect your right to your beliefs and if this is your posture, you may want to close the book, as this is the final chapter of the book.

But we say with absolute conviction, this next part of the book is the "secret sauce" to *Triumphant Transitions*. If your journey with us ends here, we sincerely thank you for choosing our book. We are keenly aware that there are literally thousands of other books you could have purchased, but you chose this one. We sincerely pray that this book has made a rich deposit into your life that has aided you on your journey. If we can ever be of service to you, please reach out. It is with our deepest gratitude that we say thank you!

SEEKING SPIRITUAL SOLUTIONS BUILDS SUCCESS

"TRUE HAPPINESS... IS NOT ATTAINED THROUGH SELF-GRATIFICATION, BUT THROUGH FIDELITY TO A WORTHY PURPOSE."

- Helen Keller [12]

To truly understand the purpose of a created thing or being, we must seek the creator to understand the intent and true purpose. If I am of the Christian faith, this means that I must seek Elohim, the Almighty One, as we see in Genesis 1:26, He is our creator.

> 'Then GOD said, "Let Us make man in Our image, according to Our likeness; let them have dominion over the fish of the sea, over the birds of the air, and over the cattle, over all the earth and over every creeping thing that creeps on the earth"'
>
> **Genesis 1:26, NKJV**

To better understand the text in Genesis 1:26,

which will help us better discern and understand our own purpose, let's look closer at some of those words in context:

man = in Hebrew means 'mankind' versus a male; referring to the human species; it is a plural, a gender neutral word

image = in Hebrew means to have the characteristics and qualities of

likeness = in Hebrew means to function like

dominion = in Hebrew means to rule, govern, master, manage, control, be the sovereign authority

So, let's put it all together:

'Then GOD said, "Let Us make mankind with our characteristics and qualities, to function like us; let them rule, govern, master, manage, control, be the sovereign authority over the fish of the sea, over the birds of the air, and over the cattle, over all the earth and over every creeping thing that creeps on the earth"'

Genesis 1:26, NKJV

We ask you to pause for a few moments, hours, or days and let that sink in. This is how Elohim created you.

Suffice it to say this gives strong evidence that you are not an accident, which means GOD birthed you into the earth on purpose. Which indicates that you have a purpose. This is part of your general purpose, but you have a specific individual purpose as well. Still not convinced? Okay, fair. Let's dig a little deeper. This is what Psalm 139:13-16 (NIV) says:

> 'For you created my inmost being; you knit me together in my mother's womb. I praise you because I am fearfully and wonderfully made; your works are wonderful, I know that full well. My frame was not hidden from you when I was made in the secret place, when I was woven together in the depths of the earth. Your eyes saw my unformed body; all the days ordained for me were written in your book before one of them came to be.'

There are numerous other verses that point to you are here "on purpose," so we hope you get the point, and if you don't, we hope you engage another believer to get better understanding.

The point is this, GOD created us with a purpose in mind. If we want to know what our purpose is, we need to be intentional to seek Him. If we do not seek GOD about our purpose the created thing (us) can be misused and abused. There is something He needs you to do. You are created on purpose. You must seek Him through prayer, studying the word, worship, and fellowship with other believers to find the trail that leads to your purpose and start pursuing it.

WATCH, WORK, PRAY

Did we say a long runway is helpful?

I know it was mentioned previously, but the point cannot be overstated. The more time you have to prepare for your transition, the better. It gives you time to think, vet your thoughts, think some more, get solid outside input, and develop a plan, which oh by the way, will need to be revised multiple times for various reasons. In addition to the impacts on you, it is also very beneficial to your family. It gives them time to come to grips with the change or to get onboard with the change. This in-turn will decrease stress on you because it will help to decrease conflict in your home.

I remember in my transition I initially felt a call to go back home to Texas. My wife wanted to go back to Florida where we had a home near the beach. As you can imagine, this caused a bit of conflict or shall I say, "intense fellowship." We kept talking and I kept praying for clarity to make sure I was hearing correctly. Then one day my wife told me that she was onboard with a transition to Texas. I almost fell out of my chair. We began to talk and plan. This led to a trip to Dallas prior to my retirement to take a look around. It was a good trip and we both felt more comfortable with the plan afterwards, although I did not have a job nor a prospect of a job at that moment.

A week or two after we had been back from our visit, I heard pretty clearly that we were not to go to Texas. My blessing was in South Carolina. A feeling of terror gripped my heart for a moment. I thought, *LORD the woman you gave me just got on board with a move to Texas and now You want me to tell her we need to stay in South Carolina? How am I going to explain this? She is going to think I don't know what the heck is going on, which will increase her stress and anxiety in this situation.* I eventually composed myself and had the conversation.

She didn't cuss or throw anything at me. Over the next few weeks, the LORD began to speak to her too and she could see what I saw, even though she didn't necessarily like it. Although she was supportive, there was some extra stress placed on her as my runway was a little short. My last day on Active duty was August 31, 2017. I did not get a phone call for an interview for the position I had been preparing for until August 29, 2017. In my heart, I knew if I got an interview the job would be mine, I still did not have employment, and this put extra stress on my family. Did I mention that it is helpful to have a long runway?

ABRUPT CHANGE

You may not have a lot of control over the runway length, which means the change will be abrupt. Acknowledge this and deal with it accordingly. This means you must be keenly aware that your stress level will be high in addition to those in your home. This can lead to arguments, children being more emotional, or you being short-tempered. The bottom line is, you have to stop and check the temperature of your home more often to ensure the engine doesn't blow up. It will undoubtedly be stressful, but with constant check-ins and adjustments to the plan, it too shall pass. I am a living witness. The constant check-ins and adjustments are vital to the process.

Why are constant check-ins vital? Your body and mind are no different than a car engine. If I were to drive my car down the road at 6,000 RPMs for 6 hours consecutively, there is a good chance that I might blow my car engine up. You are no different. Running at high levels of stress can lead to ulcers, high blood pressure, anxiety, hives, rashes, fibromyalgia, gastritis, migraines, panic attacks, etc. The human body was not designed to be in fight or flight mode for extended periods of time. This is caused by the hormone Cortisol flooding our bodies. This is the hormone that gives humans that energy and strength to prevail in dangerous situations when life and limb is on the line.

DAILY READING OF SACRED TEXT

One way I kept my stress level down was by having daily quiet time to read my sacred text, which for me is the Bible. By spending time daily in the Word, I was reminded of how much my GOD loved me and the lengths He went to show me that He loved me. I would read promises that would give me daily booster shots to walk out my faith.

My mind would start off all over the map when I would start reading, but eventually, I would lose myself in the text and my spirit would be open to the voice of GOD and then I would get instructions. This was extremely critical in me walking out my faith that this particular position was where I was supposed to be. The good LORD would drop crumbs for me to follow. He would provide just enough to get me through the day and then I would be right back at His feet.

This helped to keep me steady and calm. This helped me to keep my house calm. If you look back through my journal there are probably at least 100 scriptures that I highlighted during that period of time that gave me great comfort. The two that resonated the most were Isaiah 26:3-4 and Isaiah 42:16. These verses carried me on numerous mornings when I felt unsure. They empowered me to take another step when I didn't know what lay ahead.

Studying the Word also gave me lots of practical wisdom in navigating the circumstances. Whatever your faith may be, if you have one, I am confident your sacred text will be a wellspring of wisdom that will help you to navigate your course and provide you with comfort. For me, this was the Bible. There is one text in particular that speaks to owing no one anything. Up to this point I had not lived by those instructions, and boy did it create some unwanted stress. Since my runway wasn't really long and I did not get a call for a phone interview until just before my active-duty service ended, I had to shoulder a lot of stress. This spilled over to my wife as well. If I did not have any debt, the stress level would have gone down significantly.

JOURNALING

Journaling was a way that I could de-stress and refocus. It allowed me time to discern reality from my imagination. It also helped me to put things in perspective. Sometimes I would get really spun up over a perceived hurdle I was facing, and journaling helped me to see things for what they actually were. This was huge! If journaling is not your thing, I highly encourage you to find some other method to take 10-minutes a day to mitigate your stress level. Stress is inevitable, but we must be intentional not to let stress turn into distress.

Journaling was also a significant help in navigating my way through my transition. I would often get nuggets from day to day and individually they would not always lead to any significant revelation, but in the aggregate they often would. I made it a habit to read the previous month's journal entries prior to beginning the new month. This allowed me to see growth, receive course corrections and uncover nuggets of wisdom that enabled me to make the proper moves at the necessary times.

It also helped me to better explain how I felt as I had previously fleshed out my thoughts and by being able to articulate how I felt to those in my circle, I was able to continue to regulate my stress levels instead of letting stress regulate me. Most importantly, I was able to capture my prayers and then see how GOD answered my prayers. This encouraged my faith and kept me moving forward one step at a time, despite not knowing exactly where the path would lead.

PRAYER

What is prayer? Prayer is simply communication between you and your maker. It does not require any fancy language or any particular posture. All it requires is open and honest communication, which involves listening too. For myself, and I am confident it was the same for HH, this was a critical part of the process.

Prayer kept me sane, focused, and encouraged. In prayer, I was able to release all of my fears and doubts and receive divine instructions and encouragement. It was in prayer where I could be completely honest about every single concern that popped into my head. This was cathartic and therapeutic, and it prevented me from overwhelming my wife with a million thoughts that would have potentially overloaded her system as she had her own breathtaking load of thoughts about the transition.

It was in prayer, where I received a lot of answers. Now to be clear, I did not pray one minute and receive an answer in the next.

Sometimes it was a week or two or four or a couple of months after I prayed before I received an answer. But each day, regardless of if I had received answers or not, I fellowshipped with my Father in Heaven.

This daily fellowship really kept me grounded, which helped me to keep my wife grounded, because if I would have been all over the place in a constant state of frenzy, she would have potentially fed off of this and that would not have been good for my household. Transition is difficult enough; we did not need an extra layer of self-created drama to go on top of it. I believe that my daily seeking of the Father made it clear that I was dependent on Him and seeking Him in my transition because I made Him a priority every day. This led to Him being present and active in the transition. There are a couple scriptures that speak to this:

> "And you will seek Me and find Me, when you search for Me with all your heart."
>
> **Jeremiah 29:13 (NKJV)**

"I love those who love me, and those who seek me find me."

Proverbs 8:17 (NIV)

"Ask, and it shall be given you; seek, and ye shall find; knock, and it shall be opened unto you."

Matthew 7:7 (KJV)

"And GOD is able to bless you abundantly, so that in all things at all times, having all that you need, you will abound in every good work."

2 Corinthians 9:8 (NIV)

In my ancient text it states that GOD knows the end from the beginning (Isaiah 46:10) and so if I believe this, then He knows what I need to do to be successful. This means if I am on the wrong path, He can put me on the right path. It also means if I am on the right path, He will provide the instructions I need to get to my destination (Isaiah 42:16). He knows the people I need to meet and will give me favor with them or those around them (Proverbs 3:1-4). If I believe all of these things are true, why would I not seek Him out every day, and not just while in transition?

STEPS ARE ORDERED

Now if I believe the previous paragraph is true, then I believe my steps are ordered by GOD (Psalms 37:23), then what is holding me back?

> "Delight thyself also in the LORD; and he shall give thee the desires of thine heart. Commit thy way unto the LORD; trust also in him; and he shall bring [it] to pass...The steps of a [good] man are ordered by the LORD: and he delighteth in his way."
>
> **Psalms 37:4-5, & 23 (KJV)**

For those familiar with these passages of Scripture, how many times has it been assessed as a person's hopes, dreams and wishes being granted as a way to get ahead. It is a great encouragement and a pretty good source of joy. It even preaches well. But is that what is meant?

I offer that, for me, GOD implanted the desire to be a town manager to the central part of my thoughts. It really did play in a way that was beyond my original thoughts and intentions. Let me play it back for you, essentially how my steps were ordered, or guided in this direction.

I could take you back to an earlier point in my career, but I'll spare you. Let's go back to 2015. I was encouraged to strive to become a Command Chief Master Sergeant, of which I had no interest. In 2016, I was interviewed by my boss about why I did not want to be a Command Chief. My name was submitted, and I was selected as a candidate.

Still not excited about the potential, I put my name in the ring for another opportunity. Meanwhile I had many interviews that resulted in my non-selection, which I took as a sign of me being on the right track of not becoming a Command Chief. That is, until I was interviewed with an installation commander in Massachusetts. This leader hired me as a Command Chief and my path was set for me.

The things I learned and was exposed to would reshape my perspectives regarding community leadership roles, value, and impacts. During this time, the idea was birthed in me to find out what my responsibility could be compared to, which led me to have interest in this level of management. My job as the Command Chief connected me with municipal leaders that later encouraged and empowered my transition into the role I have now.

My steps were ordered, I was led into this profession beyond my intent and imagination. By tracing my steps backwards, I can see the path that led me to this point.

Can you recognize the leading and prompting in your life? Is there a direction, or redirection, that is beyond your self-ambition? What could happen if you followed that lead? Will you walk in faith on a path that is paved for you?

DEFEAT DOUBLE-MINDEDNESS

Once you fight past double-mindedness, this becomes a critical daily routine to ensure you do not slip back into double-mindedness. It also helps to guard against "firefighters" who purposefully or inadvertently cast doubt onto the vision you see. This is not to say that you do not need people to vector you and give you a reality check, but you do not need to be surrounded by a bunch of people who are negative.

You have to keep in mind that it is your vision and not a collective vision. Others won't see it because it is not for them. Additionally, if you do not constantly rehearse what you see in your mind's eye you will get busy and forget. When you forget, you allow the cares of life to consume you and the next thing you know the window of opportunity has passed. You must be decisive and intentional to remember what you see. In fact, we encourage you to rehearse it and rehearse it until everywhere you look, it is all you see and think about.

One way to rehearse what you see is to use

affirmations. Affirmations can be a very powerful and effective tool to help you get from where you are to where you want to be. But before we get into affirmations, let's clarify what affirmations are not. They are not a magical formula to help bring a fantasy to pass. Affirmations are not a shortcut to the destination of success.

Affirmations are a verbal rehearsal of what you see in your mind. Affirmations add words to the picture in your head. When you have a crystal-clear picture in your head of what you desire and you add the verbal picture, you are now empowering your conscious mind and your subconscious mind to go to work to help you achieve your desired end state. And from a spiritual perspective, the releasing of your words into the atmosphere starts the process of the atmosphere delivering to you everything you desire.

Psalm 103:20 says that GOD's angels are listening for His commands. When you are a child of the King, and you have a clear vision of His plan for your life and you align your words with His, the angels go to work on your behalf. I cannot say where or when it will show up, but I can assure you that it will show up. This force has brought people into my life who had the influence or resources to help bring about the vision.

Affirmations also help as they will restrict your activities to the vision. If you do not rehearse the vision daily, you will likely say yes to giving your time and energy to things that are good, but don't align with the vision. This is sacrificing great for good. Rehearsing the vision with affirmations helps to better establish a right and left boundary.

It restricts our activities to the things that are most important. From a spiritual perspective, Proverbs 29:18 (NASB) states, "Where there is no vision, the people are unrestrained." Daily rehearsing verbally what you see ensures the main thing stays the main thing. As an example, as I got closer to the time when I was going to transition, I had to start handing off to others some things that I enjoyed doing, so I could focus on what I saw as my future. I didn't want to, but I had to. And it seemed as if the closer I got to my transition, the more things that popped up in front of me to distract me toward the "good" but did not align with my future.

VICTORY LAPS

It is written that every good and perfect gift comes from above (James 1:17). After you have gone through the arduous process and made a triumphant transition, as a believer you have to give all of the glory for your transition to GOD. He is the creator of everything and is the one who endowed you with your gifts and talents. Why would you not point people to Him? It is by His grace, mercy, and favor that you arrive at your next station in life. The Bible says that GOD opens doors that no man can shut and that He closes doors that no man can open (Isaiah 22:22 & Revelations 3:7-9).

If we are honest, we must acknowledge there were doors that were opened that had nothing to do with our effort. It was GOD's favor going before us to open the doors. So, what do we mean by GOD's favor going before you to open a door? When someone is in their office and your name suddenly pops into their mind and they are prompted to do something on your behalf, without you asking, this is GOD's favor going before you. When you go through the interview process and you do not have one thing they have listed as a requirement, but they say, "There was something about you," that is GOD's favor going before you. When someone randomly introduces you to a person of influence and the way they speak of you makes you blush because they really paint you in a very positive light, that is GOD's favor going before you. Proverbs 3:1-4 (KJV) says:

> My son, do not forget my law, but let your heart keep my commands; For length of days and long life And peace they will add to you. Let not mercy and truth forsake you; Bind them around your neck, Write them on the tablet of your heart, And so find favor and high esteem In the sight of GOD and man.

It has been our experience that when we give GOD the glory that it initiates a positive cycle of more blessings. It looks something like this: (1) We acknowledge HIM and seek HIM for direction in life and how to live; (2) The more we spend time with HIM the more our lives start to look like Him; (3) His favor goes before you to open doors;

(4) You walk through the door and give Him the glory; (5) He loves it and sends more blessings.

It is just like when your kid comes in and lays it on thick about how you are the best parent, and they love and adore you. Your heart starts to swell and the next thing you know, you are off to get some ice cream or to the mall, depending on their age. Our Abba Father in Heaven is no different, lest we forget that we are made in His image (Genesis 1:26).

SCRIPTURE FOR MEDITATION

The following scriptures were very helpful and encouraging to us in our journey. We hope that they are a blessing to you as well. We encourage you to spend a lot of time reading and meditating on them. They are not a magic formula that works when you say them three times, but when you take the time to let them really get into your heart and spirit, they become rocket fuel for success. They help you successfully navigate the challenging times of your transitions, and yes there will be challenging times. They will help you to navigate treacherous waters and slippery rocks on a narrow mountain pass. What they will ultimately do, if you spend time in them, is draw you deeper into the heart of the Father. And when in His presence, we find everything we need.

"Thou wilt shew me the path of life: in thy presence is fullness of joy; at thy right hand there are pleasures for evermore."

Psalm 16:11 (KJV)

"I will instruct you and teach you in the way you should go; I will guide you with My eye."

Psalm 32:8 (NKJV)

"As for me, I will call upon GOD, And the LORD shall save me. Evening and morning and at noon I will pray, and cry aloud, And He shall hear my voice."

Psalm 55:16 (NKJV)

"Cause me to hear Your lovingkindness in the morning, For in You do I trust; Cause me to know the way in which I should walk, For I lift up my soul to You."

Psalm 143:8 (NKJV)

"Trust in the LORD with all your heart And do not lean on your own understanding. In all your ways acknowledge Him, And He will make your paths straight."

Proverbs 3:5-6 (NKJV)

"Depend on the LORD in whatever you do, and your plans will succeed."

Proverbs 16:3 (NCV)

"The Spirit of the LORD shall rest upon Him, The Spirit of wisdom and understanding, The Spirit of counsel and might, The Spirit of knowledge and of the fear of the LORD."

Isaiah 11:2 (NKJV)

"You will keep him in perfect peace, Whose mind is stayed on You, Because he trusts in You. Trust in the LORD forever, For in YAH, the LORD, is everlasting strength."

Isaiah 26:3-4 (NKJV)

"The grass withers, the flower fades, But the word of our GOD stands forever."

Isaiah 40:8 (NKJV)

"For I am the LORD your GOD who takes hold of your right hand and says to you, Do not fear; I will help you."

Isaiah 41:13 (NIV)

"I will go before you And make the crooked places straight; I will break in pieces the gates of bronze And cut the bars of iron."

Isaiah 45:2 (NKJV)

"I will bring the blind by a way they did not know; I will lead them in paths they have not known. I will make darkness light before them, And crooked places straight. These things I will do for them, And not forsake them."

Isaiah 42:16 (NKJV)

"The LORD GOD has given Me The tongue of the learned, That I should know how to speak A word in season to him who is weary. He awakens Me morning by morning, He awakens My ear To hear as the learned."

Isaiah 50:4 (NKJV)

"Call to Me, and I will answer you, and show you great and mighty things, which you do not know."

Jeremiah 33:3 (NKJV)

"Are not five sparrows sold for two copper coins? And not one of them is forgotten before GOD. But the very hairs of your head are all numbered. Do not fear therefore; you are of more value than many sparrows."

Luke 12:6-7 (NKJV)

Ask, and it will be given to you; seek, and you will find; knock, and it will be opened to you. For everyone who asks receives, and he who seeks finds, and to him who knocks it will be opened. Or what man is there among you who, if his son asks for bread, will give him a stone? Or if he asks for a fish, will he give him a serpent? If you then, being evil, know how to give good gifts to your children, how much more will your Father who is in heaven give good things to those who ask Him!

Matthew 7:7-11 (NKJV)

"And He said to me, 'My grace is sufficient for you, for My strength is made perfect in weakness.' Therefore most gladly I will rather boast in my infirmities, that the power of Christ may rest upon me."

2 Corinthians 12:9 (NKJV)

"Now to Him who is able to do exceedingly abundantly above all that we ask or think, according to the power that works in us."

Ephesians 3:20 (NKJV)

Be anxious for nothing, but in everything by prayer and supplication, with thanksgiving, let your requests be made known to GOD; and the peace of GOD, which surpasses all understanding, will guard your hearts and minds through Christ Jesus. Finally, brethren, whatever things are true, whatever things are noble, whatever things are just, whatever things are pure, whatever things are lovely, whatever things are of good report, if there is any virtue and if there is anything praiseworthy—meditate on these things.

Philippians 4:6–8 (NKJV)

"And my GOD shall supply all your needs according to His riches in glory by Christ Jesus."

Philippians 4:19 (NKJV)

A PRAYER FOR OUR READERS

LORD GOD Almighty, we come to You in deep appreciation for not just what has been done for us, but for how this collective work will reach, inform, encourage, empower, and inspire others. We anticipate that every reader, and those that they engage with this information will be abundantly blessed in every transition type in their lives. May they find a relationship with You as primary, and may they have favor with GOD and man as a result of their faith, faithfulness and efforts extended.

Father, we ask that Your hand be upon them, Your spirit speak to them, and they have what it takes to put the principles and appropriate actions in place within their lives. Like Nehemiah, give them a mind to work and provide the strength and energy required. For some it will be exciting and fun, even in times of uncertainty. For others, we ask that You bring peace beyond their understanding during the processes.

Use these people, we pray, regardless of stage of life, ethnicity, physical abilities, socio-economic background, and functional areas of experience and expertise to advance in life and represent You along the way. And for those with cognitive challenges, we pray for miracles and healing, so that rapid recovery and advancements place them in positions to have triumphant transitions beyond what others may have thought!

We adore You, LORD, for the insight and time to collaborate, now we ask that the things given to us be put into the hands of people all over the world with notable results following.

We release this work and these people into Your loving arms. Have Your way. In Jesus' name, amen!

ENDNOTES

1. Commit Works. "Everyone Has a Plan Until They Get Punched in the Mouth - Commit Works." www.commit.works, March 26, 2020. https://www.commit.works/everyone-has-a-plan-until-they-get-punched-in-the-mouth/.

2. Twitter, March 30, 2019. https://twitter.com/jackcanfield/status/1112036841417572352.

3. "Visualization." Merriam-Webster.com Dictionary, Merriam-Webster, https://www.merriam-webster.com/dictionary/visualization. Accessed 2 Nov. 2021.

4. (US Constitution, 1776).

5. Shakespeare, W. (1623). *Measure for Measure*.

6. Vora, Tanmay. "On Leadership and Dealing with Comfortable Inaction | QAspire." QAspire | Leveraging the Power of Visual Thinking to Build Better Leaders and Learners | Sketchnotes India.qaspire.com, February 21, 2011. https://qaspire.com/2011/02/21/on-leadership-and-dealing-with-comfortable-inaction/.

7. Oldster, Kilroy J. Essay. In Dead Toad Scrolls. Bradenton, FL: BOOKLOCKER.COM, 2016.

8. Gordon, Jon. Essay. In Training Camp: What the Best Do Better than Everyone Else: A Fable about Excellence. Hoboken, NJ: John Wiley & Sons, 2009.

9. "Guard." Merriam-Webster.com Dictionary, Merriam-Webster, https://www.merriam-webster.com/dictionary/guard. Accessed 1 Nov. 2021.

10. "Networking." Merriam-Webster.com Dictionary, Merriam-Webster, https://www.merriam-webster.com/dictionary/networking. Accessed 1 Nov. 2021.

11. Ali, Muhammad, and Ali, Hana. *The Soul of a Butterfly: Reflections on Life's*

Journey. New York, NY: 2013.

12. Keller, Helen, and Jack Belck. *The Faith of Helen Keller: The Life of a Great Woman, with Selections from Her Writings.* Kansas City, MO: Hallmark Editions, 1967.

ABOUT THE AUTHORS

HENRY L. HAYES JR.

Henry is the son of an Army veteran. He was born in Germany, moved to several locations and finished high school in Columbus, Georgia. The wisdom and loving kindness poured into him by his parents, Henry Sr. and Gwen, equipped him to join the United States Air Force at the age of 17, where he subsequently served less than two months shy of 30 years.

Throughout his military career he filled a myriad of roles, including aircraft structural maintenance craftsman, additional-duty First Sergeant, Academic Affairs, Command First Sergeant/Functional Manager, and Installation Command Chief Master Sergeant. His assignments included bases in Texas, California, Utah, Georgia, Alabama, the Pentagon, Maryland, Virginia, and Massachusetts, as well as other temporary assignments. Henry also served overseas in Japan and was deployed three times, in support of Operation "IRAQI FREEDOM" and Operation "ENDURING FREEDOM." He has influenced other military forces from Japan, England, Israel, Spain, and Africa regarding aircraft maintenance and leadership development principles.

After his transition from the Air Force, he was hired as a Town Manager in Massachusetts, where he served as the Chief Administrative Officer for the professional staff as well as served and advised the senior elected governing body, the Select Board. In this role, he set and executed a $100+ million budget, and oversaw 19 departments, rendering all aspects of municipal services to the nearly 19,000 population community. His local government career began in April 2020, at the onset of the global pandemic, COVID-19. Henry's passion for enhancing others at a community level was fulfilled with this amazing opportunity.

Henry has earned two bachelor's degrees, in applied management and Biblical studies and theology. He built upon the foundation of two associate's degrees, in human resources and airframe technology. He also possesses a Certificate in Local Government Leadership & Management and other strategic and executive courses. He has the honor of being the coordinating co-author for the book, *SILENCE, Rediscovering Your Need for Moments of Solitude*. Henry is married to Stephanie, and they have four loving children: Heather, Harmoni, Shania, and Jaylan.

CHRISTOPHER H. MCKINNEY SR.

Chris is from the small town of Luling, Texas. He was raised by his stepfather, David Miles, and his mother, Vivian Cubit. His grandparents, Cleveland Sr. and De Etta McKinney, were also a huge part of his life along with a very extensive extended family network. At the age of 18 after graduating high school he entered the U.S.A.F.

Chris was trained as a meteorologist, and he served in various meteorological positions and leadership roles. He also served through four combat tours of duty in Bosnia-Herzegovina, Iraq, and Afghanistan. His final duty station was at the 20th Fighter Wing, Shaw Air Force Base, South Carolina, where he served in the role of Installation Command Chief Master Sergeant. He was responsible for the training and professional development of 8,500+ military personnel and the morale and welfare of over 31,000 families and retirees at the Nation's largest F-16 combat fighter wing in the Combatant Air Forces. After 30-years of service, he retired in September 2017.

Chris was hired as the Executive Director of Santee-Lynches Regional Council of Governments (COG) in October 2017. In this role, he oversees the strategic vision and all assistance provided to four-county and 12 cities and towns. He has a staff of 28 and is responsible for the stewardship of a

$8.1 million budget. Through collaboration, he seeks to find and create regional efficiencies and priorities, while proactively identifying challenges and developing creative regional solutions.

He has a Master of Science Degree in Organizational Leadership, a Bachelor of Arts Degree in Business Management (Leadership Focus), and an Associate Degree in Meteorology. He is married to Danya, and they have a beautiful, blended family of six: Chanel, Jamal, Khalil, Kareem, Khloe, Christopher Jr., and four grandchildren.

9 781685 562984